Monkey Mountain Madness

Monkey Mountain Madness

Jeanne Phillips

University of Idaho Press
Moscow, Idaho
1996

Published by the University of Idaho Press
Moscow, Idaho 83844–1107
Printed in the United States of America

Design by Tamara Shidlauski

Typography by WolfPack

00   99   98   97   96   5   4   3   2   1

Library of Congress Cataloging-in-Publication Data

Phillips, Jeanne, 1926–
    Monkey mountain madness / Jeanne Phillips.
        p.   cm.   — (Living the West)
    ISBN 0-89301-192-4 (cloth.)
    1. Phillips, Jeanne, 1926–   . 2. Montana—Biography. I.
Title. II. Series.
CT275.P52984A3   1996
978.6′033′092—dc20
    [B]   95-49114
                                                            CIP

Contents

I
Weak Moment
Meets Impulsive Notion

Whatever possessed me to get off the bus in Montana on that fall day in 1970 remains a mystery to me.

Maybe it was the stupor I had fallen into gazing at the monotonous dun-colored stretches of eastern Washington, in a horrid limbo halfway between waking and sleeping. When at last the sun poised itself on a mountain peak like a red Day-Glo ball, I curled up on the seat and tried to sleep. That worked out well for about three minutes, and then a quartet of flower children in tie-dyed shirts and bell-bottomed jeans burst into song, loudly and off-key. The air brakes added their sibilant gasp to the din and the bus slowed, swung smartly into a narrow alley, and parked behind the depot.

"Missoula," the driver called. "Be here about ten minutes, folks."

The door wheezed open and a blast of cold fresh air hit me, and suddenly I couldn't stand to be on that bus another minute. A premonition bade me take along my suitcase and I stepped off to pace restlessly up and down the parking lot. By the time the other passengers were climbing back on, clutching styrofoam cups of coffee and sucking hard on their cigarettes (for people were still allowed to smoke on buses in those days), I was not of a mind to get back on board.

"Maybe I'll stop over here for a day," I said to the driver, as though inviting him to talk me out of it.

"You sure about that?" he asked, gray eyes conveying just what he thought of whimsical people who broke their trips in the middle.

"Yes, I'm sure," I said, showing him my ticket.

He took it, looked suspiciously at both sides, and initialed the ticket for the layover. When he handed it back, I jammed it carelessly into my pocket, although I may as well have thrown it away then and there, for I never made it to my destination—southwestern Minnesota. Instead I proceeded to do a foolish and dangerous thing which I ever afterward tried to attribute to my travel-frayed condition, it being hard to admit, even to yourself, that you are subject to "reckless spells."

With no plans beyond a meal and a bed, I started down the street just as the Bitterroots swallowed the sun and its final rays were blotted up by a murky, quick-descending twilight. In the space of a blink all surfaces bathed in light changed color as well as aspect, a transformation eerie enough to disorient someone sitting in a familiar living room, let alone an exhausted wayfarer without reservations in a strange town— strange but not entirely unknown.

Shivering in the autumnal chill of a land much colder and dryer than the one I had left, I paused before a long L-shaped building that nudged at my memory.

"That's the motel where we stayed on our way to Yellowstone," I thought. "They've painted it panty pink, and tacked a dinky restaurant onto the front of it."

In spite of the vacancy sign's throbbing orange invitation, only two of the rooms appeared to be occupied. Plenty of time to check in if they started to fill up while I was eating.

The cafe was a no-nonsense establishment, deserted except for three people, one of whom I took to be the waitress since she wore a grungy white uniform and businesslike oxfords. She was sitting at one of the four tables, bent over a newspaper, her right index finger crooked through the handle of a nearly empty coffee cup. Beside the cup was half a doughnut on a turquoise plastic saucer.

When the door shut behind me she looked up, popped the rest of the doughnut into her mouth, and produced a pencil from somewhere in the recesses of her teased-up, iron-gray hair. As though anticipating big doings, she dug a jackknife out of one pocket, flipped it open, and began to sharpen the pencil.

At the counter two middle-aged men sipped coffee from white mugs, their dirty dinner plates shoved to one side and receiving a going over from some ambitious flies. I paid the men scant attention until one of them said, "Huh! You gotta be kidding, Dick, and you the great-grandson of Rowdy Joe Lowe?"

I looked up from the menu I'd been scanning (a fancy four-pager totally at odds with the bare-bones cafe). Rowdy Joe was a saloon keeper described by historians as a particularly odious procurer and murderer, yet this Lowe looked fairly harmless . . . had the generations between diluted that wild blood? The men lowered their voices to a murmur and I heard no more.

The waitress came over to take my order, although it was plain from her expression that she had no use for outlanders. Still, a glint of curiosity flashed in her eyes as she studied my rumpled pants and the coffee stain down the front of my coat, the result of a brake-stomping near-accident just outside of Coeur d'Alene.

"We ain't got no quiche or Perrier," she said gruffly, "to save ya' the trouble of asking."

"No wonder there's only two people in here," I said, "and they're probably your relatives."

Instead of booting me out, she seemed pleased. She actually smiled, putting several cracks in her heavy, buff-toned makeup, and asked me what I wanted. After she had gone I turned back to the men, my mood considerably lightened by the purse-lipped way she had hissed "kwitchy" for quiche.

Dick Lowe was now sitting sideways on the stool talking rapidly while one work-gnarled hand flew up and down in a chopping motion. His hawkish profile, under the pale-gray Stetson, wasn't really handsome, but his vitality had an attraction of its own.

Both men grinned at a shared bit of humor, and a deep scar-like crease appeared momentarily beneath Dick's high, flat cheekbone. Unruly dark sideburns, flecked with gray, reached down to meet the upturned collar of his sheepskin-lined jacket. My eyes moved down the olive-drab work pants to his feet, which I expected to find encased in cowboy boots. Instead he wore scuffed black loafers, the right one tapping the floor with an inexorable rhythm. A rush of giggles rose in my throat for no good reason, and the all-gone feeling I'd experienced on the bus blew away in the hot air generated as the two tossed brag around.

Halfway through my salad I glanced over at the motel. Business was still slow. Directly in my line of vision was the door to Unit 7, where my children and I had spent a night on our first vacation as a family of three after all those years as a foursome. My mind backed hastily away from that—all the way back to the days when the boys were small, and it didn't matter where my husband and I went on vacation, just so we were together . . . days when we were as close as two people can be. Was such happiness worth the pain that followed?

This bittersweet rumination continued until the waitress returned with a big white oval platter covered with a slab of chicken-fried steak. When I had nearly bested the hunk of cow, Lowe's friend got up and sauntered out of the restaurant, and without so much as a "by your leave" Lowe slid off the stool and came over to my table. I couldn't recall that he had even glanced at me when I came in, or at any time since, but he pulled out the other chair and sat down across from me.

"So," he said, "how are things on the road these days?"

I shrugged and cut off my next-to-last bite of steak. It would take a better opening than that to lure me into conversation. The eyes of the waitress glared like headlights; I wondered what emotion had caused the icy-gray gleam.

My luggage was on the floor beside me, and Lowe reached down to flip over the I.D. tag hanging from the strap.

"How do you pronounce that?" he asked.

"Oh, just call me Jenny . . . most everyone does . . . and you're Dick? That's what your friend called you."

"Yep. Middle name's Richard. I don't use my first name."

I waited for him to tell me what it was, but he continued to stare at the printing on the luggage tag as though it were a hieroglyphic that would reveal what made me tick if he could just decipher it.

A blond in a green smock walked out of the kitchen, smiled at Dick, and slipped a coin into one of the oldest jukeboxes outside of a museum. After some whirring and clicking, and a clunk like a dropped rock, a truculent voice yelled out something about the old man from the mountain.

"Do you like to dance?" Dick asked. I could hear his feet moving under the table, one tapping and one shuffling, like a kid trying to pat his head and rub his stomach at the same time.

I nodded and wiped up the last smear of gravy with a crust of bun I had almost overlooked. Glancing up, I caught such a kindly expression of concern on his face that the sketchy inner resources I still possessed promptly deserted me. He quickly replaced the sympathetic look with a noncommittal half smile, but the damage had already been done, and I began to babble about my dissatisfaction with my present life—or lack of one, you might say.

Dick nodded or said "uh-huh" from time to time, and when the notion occurred to me that I might enjoy spending some time on a dude ranch, I blurted that out too. His head snapped up like an old war-horse's at the sound of bugles.

"Ranch?" he cried. "You want *ranch?* I'll give you ranch! Why I'm caretaker at the most *fantastic* . . . a millionaire's play ranch, up in the mountains southeast of here. A summer retreat. Why, it's just . . . it . . ."

He began to stammer, at a loss to adequately describe the splendor of the place. I picked up my bill.

"Isn't that nice," I said, taking money out of my wallet.

Dick untangled his tongue and said, "Of course, I don't live in the main lodge. They fixed up the original homesteader's log cabin for the help's quarters."

Log cabin. Original. The words hung in the air between us like temptation incarnate, as my common sense followed my inner resources out the door. And oh wasn't Dick swift to notice how my coffee cup wavered halfway to my mouth, dribbling coffee to the tablecloth. I saw born in his eyes the idea that he would take me home with him, as surely as he must have perceived the helpless consent already burning in mine.

The waitress got up, dimmed the lights, and began to tug heavy draperies across the window.

"Closing up now?" I asked.

She bobbed her head and turned away, and Dick stood up. I experienced a thrill of panic as some remnant of my brain still functioning reminded me he hadn't *actually* invited me to do this insane thing which

I was about to do. At that point I couldn't have said whether I was more concerned about the notion of going or about being left behind with thoughts of unvisited historical sites torturing my mind.

"Is that all you brought with you?" he asked, gesturing at my suitcase.

"Yes," I said. "Listen, I . . . ah . . . hope you don't think . . ."

"Don't worry. I won't bother you," he said, hoisting my suitcase and walking out. I trailed along, and when the door had closed behind us he added, "it's just that the loneliness gets to me sometimes, Jenny. Even a day or two of company would mean an awful lot to me."

When Dick opened the door of his truck the overhead light revealed deep crevasses that time or the elements, or both, had carved in his lean cheeks—the marks of hard living that the dim restaurant lighting had concealed. He was older than I'd thought, and I was not displeased to see it.

We talked very little after that, other than a few remarks about the weather and climate, and by the time we whizzed past Clinton I was beginning to wonder just where this alleged play ranch was located. It hardly seemed to be where wealthy people would build a retreat, and before long my mother's voice had sneaked into my head and was inquiring in snide tones if I didn't think maybe I had played the idiot again. My voice reedy with escalating tension, I finally asked, "How much farther is this place?"

"We turn off just this side of those lights up ahead,"

he said. "That's Rock Creek Tavern—want to stop for a drink?"

"Oh, I don't think so," I said. "It's been a long day."

His lips drew back, thinning out until they had all but disappeared, and I figured I must have angered him to bring on such a peculiar grimace. We turned off the highway and drove past the bar. Farther down the gravel road, Dick stopped the truck before a padlocked gate and turned to me.

"That's good," he said. "To tell the truth, I was testing you. The last woman I . . . had up there was a real lush, and I never intend to go through that again."

A test, was it? I didn't much like that, but then I cared even less for the idea of hoofing it all the way back to Missoula.

"How much farther now?" I asked.

"Oh—twenty-two, twenty-three miles—as the crow flies," he said.

"But it's all up and down," I said, peering out at the mountains towering above us. Then as I pondered his words, "the last woman I had up there," some of the magic went out of the night. Maybe I was just the latest in a long string of women. But did it really matter? At least it would be a place to rest and reconnoiter.

Even before I'd gotten off the bus, I had begun to have second thoughts about this pointless trip to Minnesota, land of my birth and rearing, where I hadn't set foot since the age of seventeen. Now I abruptly decided that the whole idea had been wishful thinking—there would be no clue to my future there. I'd never been much for back-tracking anyhow, so maybe it was time

to start paying some attention to those hints my subconscious had been tossing up for the past year with
increasing urgency, and always accompanied by sign-
posts plainly pointing *north.*

Dick had gotten out to open the gate. He drove
through it, stopped, and said, "Would you mind closing it behind us? Just spin the dial a few times after you
snap the padlock."

Trying to squelch the alarming idea that he would
drive off and leave me standing in the woods, I
hopped out. He would hardly bring someone clear
from Missoula just to close the gate behind him. After
I had hauled it shut and secured the lock, I stood gazing at the sky, nearly hypnotized by the overripe gib-
bous moon that hung there. Somehow it didn't look
like the same old familiar moon. I rubbed my eyes and
looked at it again, feeling more insignificant by the
moment.

"It's beautiful," I said, climbing back into the truck.
"Been a long time since I really looked at the sky."

"Valley of the Moon Ranch, they call it," Dick said,
and a certain wistfulness in his voice suggested that he
would give his soul to have it for his own.

When we were under way again, he asked me if I
had any children.

"Yes, two boys," I said, "but they're grown and gone
now."

I could finally think about that without pain, but
actually saying the words caused a pang of longing.
The children had only recently gone, leaving my home
without a radiance I had not realized graced it until its

absence brought lackluster days and vaguely uneasy nights.

A modest inheritance had made it possible for me to resign from my job as secretary to a criminal defense attorney—a position that had, over the years, lowered my estimation of *Homo sapiens* a few notches too many for comfort. It also instilled in me the notion that people live many different lives either overtly and serially or all at once on various hidden levels. The end of summer had found me bored and acutely conscious of the need to move on to another stage of my own life. I had then spent weeks planning the trip I had jettisoned in about a minute at the cafe back in Missoula.

I pushed these thoughts aside with a sigh, and as though responding to a signal, Dick cleared his throat. But he didn't speak, and we continued on up the mountain on a twisting one-lane road bordered by towering evergreens. He didn't seem inclined to interrogate me any further about my personal life, which led me straight to the conclusion that he would prefer not to be questioned about his own. My uneasiness increased as the silence lengthened, and I began to imagine all sorts of violent scenarios, all the way from a head-on collision on the narrow road, to my lifeless body crumpled on the forest floor, green with decay and ravaged by wildlife.

As we ground up one switchback after another, I noticed stretches of road not rimmed by trees where deep chasms yawned like dark hungry maws. Leaning close to the window, I saw to my horror that the wheels of the truck couldn't have been more than a few inches from the verge. I tried to form some kind of prayer, but all that came to mind was "fools die."

"Well, we're a good two-thirds of the way," Dick said, braking to a stop. Having squeezed my eyes shut against impending disaster, I opened them to see that we had reached a plateau. On every side timbered slopes rose rank upon serried rank to mountain peaks blue-limned in the moonglow. In the center of these behemoths spearing the night sky lay a high valley.

Dick got out, presumably to answer a call of nature. He smoked part of a cigarette, the tip glowing eerily in the darkness. When he came back he removed his hat, tossed it onto the dashboard, and turned to me, face expressionless and eyes unreadable in the dim light.

"Your hair looks beautiful," he said, "with the moonlight shining on it like that."

And took me in his arms.

My composure collapsed like a straw house at the first stiff breeze, and after a couple of preliminary squawks there erupted from my throat some most unattractive bawls and squalls.

"You said," I sobbed, "you said you *wouldn't* . . ."

He let go of me so fast I fell back against the door, but his voice was calm when he said,

"Yes, Ma'am. This traveling really takes a lot out of a person. Could have driven a little faster if I'd know how played out you were, but I though you might be enjoying the scenery."

Tears continued to leak from my eyes as we bumped along toward this phantom ranch I no longer believed existed and yet I had to admit that Dick might have only intended it as a friendly hug—a welcome to his high lonesome world. And what could I expect anyway, going home with a man I had only talked to for half an hour?

Dread mushroomed into terror as Dick parked beside a log cabin that loomed up suddenly. It seemed incongruous in the middle of this virtually untracked wilderness which, as I happened to know due to years of indefatigable map-gazing, bordered on thousands of acres of National Forest. Dick got out, unlocked the door, and without a backward glance marched in, his back ramrod-stiff. He left the door ajar for me to follow or not as I chose.

The mountain air was incredibly cold. It seeped insidiously into my very bone marrow, and when it had caused a little icicle to form on the end of my nose, I gave up and went into the cabin. It seemed at first glance to be just a large rectangular room, its bachelor occupant not expecting company, for he stood at the sink hastily washing a stack of dirty dishes.

Closing the door softly behind me, I looked around. The breath I hadn't known I was holding blew out in relief when I saw the twin beds separated by a big eight-drawer bureau. Each had two fat pillows and a comforter, the sight of which caused my body to want to fold up with weariness. How long had it been since I had stretched out in a bed? My feet trotted me straight to the nearest one, which gave a loud squawk when I sagged down on it. Dick glanced over at me but didn't speak.

From there I could see part of a bathroom through an open door—an old-fashioned sink with a medicine cabinet yawning open above it, and a yellow towel lying in a heap on the linoleum beneath.

"The door at the other end of the kitchen," I said, "does it lead outside, too? I thought at first that was the bathroom."

Dick nodded and began to sweep some debris on the floor into a pile. Hardly able to suppress a groan at the ineffable comfort of lying down, I turned my back to him. Next thing I knew, someone was saying:

"Hey, I was only kidding about that door."

I flopped over to see a man standing beside me, and for one awful moment couldn't think where I was, who he was, or what on earth he could be talking about.

"Since you're bent on playing the virtuous virgin," Dick said, "you go on through that other door. You'll find another bathroom and a bedroom, and it's all yours."

I sat up groggily, examining his face for signs of pre-varication. It had been my lot in life to know a great many "kidders," most of whom would draw the line at practically nothing. For all I knew, this last declaration might be just as false as his nod when I asked if the door led outside. Another little joke, as it were.

I sidled past him, half expecting that after I'd stepped through the door he would slam and lock it behind me, leaving me out in the cold with the rest of the wild crea-tures. Very cautiously I pushed it open. My groping hand found a light switch, and I snapped it on to a blaze of polished chrome and shining surfaces. All was cleanliness and order here, from the pale green shower and window curtains to the deep-piled carpet. A trio of ceramic fish, arranged in steps on one wall, watched me with translucent eyes.

Moving on to the room beyond it, I experienced a warm sensation of coming home. The inside halves of the log walls were peeled, and in this room they were varnished and hung with numerous black-framed historical prints of early Montana.

"Look at that," I murmured, glancing at some of the titles, "Saint Ignatious Mission . . . Missoula 1865 . . ." I hastily closed both doors so Dick wouldn't think I was talking to him and follow me in. "And this rug—the genuine article, I'll bet."

The carpet glowed with the rich reds and royal blues of fine Oriental craftsmanship, and when I stopped to fold back one corner, tiny knots proved its authenticity.

A fancy brass and wrought-iron thermometer showed the temperature to be a comfortable sixty-eight degrees, and I noticed a wall heater blowing warm air into the room. Over the bed hung an artifact that could only have been a peace pipe, and the moment my eyes slid down to the orange-peel patterned quilt, the drugged feeling of sleepiness returned. Lurching to the window, I pulled open the drapes and stars seemed to leap right into the room. I opened the window an inch to pine-scented air, and as I turned back toward the bed I fancied that the heavenly aroma was working deeper into my body with every breath, soothing the hurting places like a tender hand spreading healing balm.

Without stopping to unpack I shucked shoes and outer clothing and crawled under the covers, the bed welcoming me with soft whispers of reassurance. Actually it was a rustle familiar from my childhood.

"Can you believe it?" I asked myself, smiling into the darkness. "A straw mattress."

I didn't allow myself to drift off to sleep, though, until I heard the creak of bedsprings in the other room and Dick's first soft, buzzing snores.

2
Paradise
in the Pines

Sunlight so bright it penetrated my eyelids woke me.

"Made it through the night in one piece," I mumbled, rolling over to face the inside wall. My soft utterance must have disturbed some birds perched in the tree by my window. They started up a loud scolding racket, which changed in mid-squawk as though by common consent into a thrilling concert of warbles and trills. I responded by whistling a few bars of "Under the Bamboo Tree," shocking them into silence.

I fluffed up the feather pillows, turned on my back, and gazed around the room. Why was it so lovely and the rest of the place so spartan? It must have been fixed up for someone special, and I couldn't help wondering what had become of her. I thought about Dick's comment after he had invited me to join him for a drink at Rock Creek Tavern.

"A real lush, and I never intend to go through that again."

A test, he had admitted . . . a test which I had passed, unaware of being tested. Yet I was certain the woman he had referred to wasn't the *important* one. There had to have been someone else, before the toper. What I didn't know at that time, about the ranch and the man who guarded its treasures, would have filled volumes!

Curiosity about my surrounding prodded me from the comfortable bed, and I tiptoed out to have another look at the kitchen. Fortunately I paused to pull on jeans and a sweater, for Dick was already up and taking a coffee percolator out of a cupboard. He wore only maroon and white striped boxer shorts, the legs beneath them appearing to be carved from marble posts.

He reached to turn on a faucet, and the muscles moving beneath the skin on his back reminded me of Midwestern farmers, shirtless at harvest time . . . men who worked long hours their whole lives through. Clearer than words, the delineation of Dick's upper body spoke of a life of hard labor since early childhood.

He turned and wished me a good morning, totally un-abashed at being caught in his underwear. The cruel daylight revealed every pit and scar on his face, and more—the shadowy, ineradicable nuances of past catastrophes. Yes, he was well into middle age, and I wondered if my fright of the previous night had flattered him. The amusement dancing in his brown eyes suggested as much.

"How are you this morning?" I asked, retreating before he had time to answer. Agitated by a strange excitement, I brushed my teeth with more than usual vigor, staring into my own dark eyes—eyes that offered no clue as to what wild action might germinate next in the brain behind them.

"You must be crazy," I whispered.

When I returned to the kitchen, composed and ready to accept whatever Providence might care to fling at my feet, Dick wore the same work clothes as the day before. He sat at the big round table, drinking coffee from an ochre-hued cup with "Grandpa" printed on it in brown letters. The homey word erased a great deal of my apprehension—someone's old granddad surely couldn't be a person to be feared.

"Help yourself to coffee, Jenny," he said. "Cups are in the cupboard above the sink."

When I was seated across from him, trying to choke down coffee that would have floated the Spruce Goose, he shifted his gaze out the window to watch the cumulus clouds breaking up into white crumbs as they collided with the mountain range across the valley.

"If God ever made a country more beautiful than Montana, I've never seen it," he said, "and I've done some traveling in my time."

"Is that right?" I said. "Were you a traveling salesman—or a truck driver?"

"No ma'am," he said, face puckering up as though I had insulted him. "I was a packer and wrangler . . . even rode the rodeo circuit for a while . . . Cheyenne, Pendleton, Pecos . . ."

His voice trailed off, and I got the impression that Dick had walked some dark valleys along the way.

"Could I fix you some breakfast?" I asked, my stomach growling.

"Naw, I don't eat until later on. Thanks. You go ahead and have something, and then I'll show you around the place."

He stood up and began to pace restlessly, but the morning meal was one I never skimped on if I could help it. I found eggs, kielbasa, wheat bread, and apple butter. When I had finished, we put on our coats and stepped out into a dazzle of snow and sun.

"Looks like we got a skift of snow last night," he said.

"*Skift?*"

"Yup. It might melt off in a few hours, though. Sometimes we get a few weeks of nice weather this time of year, before the real whammy hits us."

The air was delicious, and our feet crunched cheerfully on the thin layer of dry snow. When we came to the first of a group of buildings, I remarked that it looked newer than the others.

"We call that the doghouse," Dick said. "It's really the old man's office—I think he built it to lock himself in when he and missus are having a fuss."

He darted me a merry glance, suggesting he didn't take too seriously any marital tiffs his employers might engage in.

"Are they nice to work for?" I asked.

"You bet. If you didn't know different, you'd think the Finnegans were just ordinary folks."

"And they're not, I suppose, if they can afford a place like this."

"Rich as Croesus," he sighed reverently. "Now, this next little bungalow is an extra guest house, for people who don't want to stay in the main lodge for one reason or another."

I looked at the sprawling structure at the bottom of the slope.

"Eleven rooms," Dick said. "You can tell which part was the original hunting lodge and where they've added on to it to make a summer home."

"What a wonderful place to spend the summer," I said.

"Yeah, and winter's not half bad, either," he said. "Let's see—there's the garage, the granary, tool shed, tack room . . ."

"Why, it's like a small town all by itself," I exclaimed. "And what's that little hut by the river? Surely not a backhouse?"

"I can tell you're country-bred," he said, lips drawing down in his closed-mouth smile. "No, that's the sauna. The swimming pool is back behind the lodge here."

My sharply drawn breath made a whistling sound in the silence. The largest pool I had ever seen gaped at me, a few dead leaves scattered across its bottom.

"Let's sit down here for a minute," Dick said, lowering himself into a webbed chair on the stone-paved patio beside the pool. "Got sort of a stitch in my side."

I perched on an aluminum-framed chair beside him.

"Should have put this lawn furniture away weeks ago, but one of their kids stayed on longer than usual. I ought to clean and cover the pool, too, but I like to rest up for a while after they all leave."

As Dick talked, I looked beyond these man-made signs of wealth to the panorama of mountains and valley, and stretching above it all that blue sky almost too perfect to be real, like a touched-up picture in a tourist brochure. A sudden gust of elation buffeted me. *What* had I blundered into now? It almost seemed as though a chunk of Paradise had broken loose and taken root on earth.

"That's why they have to have somebody here," Dick continued. "You'll see, when we go inside—paintings, antiques, knick-knacks from all over the world—collectibles, Missus Boss calls them."

I nodded and stood up, wishing he would come on so I could see it. But Dick scratched a kitchen match on his leather hatband, continuing to sit while he smoked, and scanned the forest that grew right up to the back wall of the lodge.

"They had a man and wife working here, oh, eight or ten years ago, I guess it was," he said. "The boss said he thought they were decent people. Stayed a couple of years—but then do you know what they did?"

"No, what?" I said.

"Loaded the truck—the boss's *own truck*, mind you, with practically priceless antiques, and took off—right in the middle of winter."

Dick bent down and placed the filtered butt of his cigarette carefully under a rock. Then he looked straight at me, eyes blazing, whether with contempt for the criminals or admiration of their audacity I had no way of knowing.

"Police in seven states were looking for them," he went on, "but they may as well have disappeared into thin air."

"They never did catch them?" I asked.

"Nope, never."

Swiftly as expertly dealt cards, my mind began to present me with pictures of various places along the way where a heavily loaded truck might slip off the icy winter road and plunge into . . . thin air. Their million-dollar load might even now be lying shattered at the bottom of a deep gorge . . . but since my imagination habitually works overtime, I said nothing.

"You can be sure they checked out everyone they hired after that," Dick said. "The honor system screeched to a fast halt."

"I suppose they checked you up, down, and sideways," I said, and relaxed a little when he nodded . . . at least he couldn't be an axe murderer or something, then. He gave me another of those intent looks.

"You *will* stay, won't you, Jenny?" he asked.

I hadn't really made up my mind, but there seemed no reason not to.

"Oh, I guess so," I said. My voice didn't sound as casual as I had intended, so I added as nonchalantly as I could: "For a while, anyway."

Dick got up and we toured the lodge. The living room was dominated by a great fireplace built of river stone, and in the chill air it was easy to picture flames leaping and crackling. Around it in a semi-circle was arranged massive, comfortable-looking furniture, and the unvarnished floor of wide fir boards was scattered with faded, worn braided rugs. Behind this area was a long table with log legs, flanked by a twig rocking chair, and a strange chair constructed entirely of elk antlers.

Dick saw me looking at some discolored places on the walls. "They put the valuable oil paintings in storage, after that theft I told you about . . . only bring a few along every year, and hang them up for the summer."

He pulled a cord, and ecru drapes swished open. A buck made an odd sound of surprise before darting away and disappearing into the forest.

"Wow, the things money can buy," I said.

"Yep. But they have their problems too, just like anyone else," Dick said softly.

He didn't elaborate on the troubles of his employers.

When we had gone through about half the rooms, my impressions began to blur. It was just too much to take in all at once, and the high altitude was making me feel giddy.

"Shall we save the rest for another time?" I said. "I seem to be getting a little short on breath."

"Oh, sure. I always forget it takes some adjustment when you're not used to this thin air."

We returned to the cabin, and I fixed Dick an omelet involving cheese, sautéed onions, and chopped red peppers. After making short work of it, he announced that he was going down to the garage and attach the snow-plow to the Bronco. He must have had a good nose for the weather, for he hadn't been gone ten minutes when the white flakes began their silent downward drift, so thickly I could hardly see beyond the window.

The dizzy sensation was still nagging at me, so I stretched out on my bed. Some time later I was wakened by the roar of a motor and made it to the window in time to see Dick drive past in the Bronco with a yellow plow turning aside the snow that had accumulated on the road. It was still falling, but the large wet flakes had given way to icy pellets.

After the noise of the engine died away a profound silence reigned, and then gradually the wilderness resumed its furtive, rustling sounds. There had been a moment of desolation after Dick left, but soon the birds were muttering in the conifers again, and I realized I was far from alone. A fat squirrel streaked across the snow, cheeks bulging with tidbits to add to its winter stores.

As I stood absorbing the wild splendor, a feeling of extra-ordinary calm came over me, and the last flush of my feverish desire to rush off to Minnesota—or some place—drained away. *Vis medicatrix naturae.*

When I roused myself to go into the kitchen, I found a note propped against the cut-glass sugar bowl on the table:

"J - am going to plow as it snows. Easier that way. If you want something to do, there's makings for meat loaf. Baked spuds would be good too. Back around seven."

Yes indeed. Okay, lady, earn your keep. Well, I could handle that, but first I intended to do some poking around. Although plain compared to my room, this part of the place certainly was not lacking in modern conveniences. The big refrigerator looked nearly new, the range somewhat older but top of the line—hooked up, I presumed by the faint telltale odor, to the propane tank outside.

There seemed to be an excess of cabinets, and I looked in all of them. They were crammed with canned goods of every description, and the last one I opened was chock-a-block with round tins of cookies stacked in neat rows.

"Someone here has a sweet tooth," I said, my voice startling in the silent room. It didn't occur to me to question why Dick had stocked enough provisions to last out a six-month siege.

I moved on to his sleeping/sitting area, which was partially divided from the kitchen by a washer and dryer. Although his quarters looked comfortable enough, they were permeated with an almost tangible aura of loneliness—a lingering ache of suffering, shed by the body at sunrise and hovering over the bed, waiting for the dark hours of night.

What kind of man could live in this isolation? My eyes fell upon a picture of an attractive brunette, and I was almost certain it hadn't been on the dresser before today. Her bemused expression suggested that she knew very well what kind of man, and would be happy to tell me if she could.

When I started to cook supper, my somber mood floated away on a groundswell of elation. I worked swiftly in the grip of euphoria, humming a bouncy tune, and when the food was in the oven I broke into song and fox-trotted around snapping my fingers. It stopped snowing, and the sun came out briefly.

Then abruptly the clouds closed in again and shadows filled the corners as daylight withdrew. There was a wild beautiful sunset featuring bands of pale pistachio, cobalt blue, and a hauntingly lovely lavender.

"No red or orange," I thought. "The air must be too pure, and the snow has settled all the dust."

I gazed at the changing sky until it was almost dark, and then paused with my hand on the light switch. There were no curtains in the room.

"As sure as I turn this light on," I fretted, "someone is going to be watching me with binoculars." (It was some time before I comprehended the distances between the ranch and other houses or people.)

As the room darkened, the peeled log walls began to look like stacks of bodies. "What would you call that singing and dancing fit I had," I asked them, "mountain madness? Or is it some kind of altitude sickness?"

They began to talk back, popping and cracking as the temperature plummeted and icy night-winds moaned like old women mourning their lost men. One of the logs had twin knot-holes that bore eerie resemblance to human eyes, and they seemed to follow me as I walked back and forth setting the table.

Suddenly there was a terrible wailing scream right outside the door. I dashed over to the opposite wall, my heart banging against my ribcage, only to hear a scraping noise along that side of the cabin. Surrounded. I went back to cower by the door, willing Dick to come home.

I was still hovering there when the sound of the four-wheel drive reached my ears, whereupon I sagged into a chair and nearly bawled with relief. Dick came through the door on a blast of frigid air, stamping snow from his boots.

"You look pale," he said. "Haven't caught a virus bug or something, have you?"

"Oh no," I squeaked, "no, I feel great. Had a real good time while you were gone."

I got the food from the oven, and we sat down to eat. My case of the willies had gone out the door when Dick came in, and I matched his gusto as we demolished every scrap of meat and potatoes in ten minutes flat. As we topped off our meal with coffee, I asked Dick why my room and bath were so opulent compared to the rest of the cabin.

"That's the cook's room," he said. "They have trouble keeping one at any salary, so they try to give all the perks they can . . . not that it does much good."

"What do you mean?" I asked. "It seems to me this would be a terrific place to work."

Dick stared into his coffee cup as though searching for a way to explain it. Finally he said,

"Not for the majority of people. They don't like the quiet, can't stand the isolation. Why, more than one of them has gone tearing off down the road, lugging her suitcase—rather walk clear to the highway and hitch-hike, than spend one more minute up here."

He belched softly and slanted a look at me.

"Not my type," he said.

And certainly not mine, either.

When the table was cleared, Dick produced an Aggravation board. I knew nothing about the game, but soon found it was aptly named. After awhile I began to suspect Dick was cheating, and none too subtly. He flaunted outrageously the rules he had showed me, clearly printed in black and white, and when I was positive I called him on it.

"Why, that's what makes it fun," he said shamelessly, stunning me into a prolonged silence during which I wondered if that sort of attitude served a person well. Had my strict upbringing been in reality a . . . *disservice*, an anchor preventing me from rising to unimaginable heights of success in this world?

My instincts rejected that. Cheating was never right—was it? At any rate, playing games with a cheat was no fun, and in fact it had no point. I pushed back my chair and stood up.

"I like to read for a while before I go to bed," I said. "Would it be okay if I borrowed a book from the library down at the lodge?"

"Sure, help yourself," he said, starting to pack up the Aggravation board. "Take the keys, and lock the back door when you're through. I forgot—must be all this excitement."

All this excitement? What did *he* find exciting? Deciding he had spoken in irony, I got my coat and a head scarf. Dick had kicked off his rubber boots and left them by the heater, and I slipped my stocking-clad feet into them.

When I stopped outside, there were two huge yellow eyes glaring at me from across the road. As I stood there like a petrified tree, they changed to bloody reddish color and disappeared with a faint scrabbling sound. My nape hairs rose, and I had to battle a mighty urge to step right back into the cabin and slam the door.

This reluctance to retreat stemmed from certain things I had seen in my explorations of Dick's end of the cabin—items that had me convinced he was a dedicated prankster. If he even *suspected* I was afraid, there would be no end to the traps he would set in attempts to scare me. I forced my feet to start walking down the hill.

I hadn't taken ten steps when there was a horrendous crash in the underbrush at the side of the road. An involuntary "*ehhh*" popped out of me and I broke into a shambling run, my feet sliding back and forth in the oversized boots. Dad had always told me that talking as I walked would keep the bears away. But there were other things big enough to make that much racket—elk, cougar, deer—and it seemed to me that talking would keep your unseen enemies apprised of your whereabouts, so I shuffled along through the snow in tense silence. Being a spooky sort of person to begin with, much given to cheap thrills and alarms, my body was vibrating like a harpstring by the time I reached the lodge.

I closed the door behind me and stood breathing deeply, and had almost calmed myself when just on the other side of that door a scream ripped the air—the same wild shriek I had heard earlier outside the cabin! I tore through the huge kitchen and dining room into the library, where I had planned to spend an hour. Now I only wanted another human body nearby, and I didn't care much whose it was. Grabbing the first book my hand fell upon, I sprinted back toward the cabin, Dick's boots making horrible flatulent sounds as I squished frantically through the snow.

Easing through the door, I stood concealed by the refrigerator until my breathing was back to normal. Then I realized I had forgotten to lock the lodge. Holding the keys together so they wouldn't clink, I stealthily slipped the key-ring onto its hook behind the door. No way in this world was I going back down there before morning!

Dick was sitting in his easy chair, leafing through a magazine.

"Did you find something that interests you?" he said.

"Uh-huh," I said, looking for the first time at the book I had in my hands. I put it down on the table and walked over beside Dick.

"What is that noise like a baby squalling?" I asked. "I heard it while you were gone, and again down by the lodge just now."

He didn't answer at once, so I added, "I've heard of tropical birds that imitate a baby's cry, but this isn't the tropics by any stretch of the imagination."

"I don't know what makes that sound, Jenny," he said. "We don't have any loons around here either, so if you hear crazy laughing don't ask me what causes it. I don't know."

Crazy laughing. Oh my. My back chilled as though someone had trailed an ice cube down it. I sat at the table and absent mindedly opened my book, which proved to be an account of pioneer life near Glendive— fascinating any other time, but I just couldn't focus. It seemed that what I was living was as interesting as anything found between the pages of a book.

The warmth and safety of the cabin, after my long hectic day, finally set my head nodding.

"Good night, Dick," I said. "I'm going to bed now."

He turned and gave me a hungry look of such sad tenderness that something long frozen within me commenced to melt, and I veered over to his chair to drop a kiss on his weathered cheek. Halfway across the kitchen I could have sworn I heard a muffled chuckle. Or had I? And if I had, what kind of man laughs at an indication of affection?

"How many times today," I ragged myself, "have you said 'what kind of man?'"

I slipped into my nightgown and laid out clean clothes for tomorrow. It was true that I had never met a man like Dick, whom I already sensed was loaded with subtlety and cat-and-mouse tendencies. The churn of my thoughts turned up Sharleen Dupree, a long-time friend who had married rich and presently was cruising the Aegean Sea in what she referred to as a floating palace. We had worked at desks that faced each other, and the Monday after the weekend Sharleen met this paragon, she hadn't even sat down before screeching at me, "There is no one on *earth* like this guy I met at the Mediterranean Room Saturday night!"

"Well . . . of course, we're all unique in some way," I had conceded, refraining from mentioning that she hadn't met all the people on earth, for purposes of comparison. The stardust spraying from her love-crazed eyes had unnerved me to the point where I began to argue that people are easily classified by type. But no, she continued to maintain with some heat that Larry was totally unlike anyone else. Now I seemed to have met one of that stripe.

"You were right, Sharl," I whispered. "There are such creatures."

I cuddled down into the bed that fit me so very well, and of which I was already inordinately fond.

3
Mark
of the Lynx

My warm gesture of the previous night was not alluded to by either of us as I devoured the bacon and eggs Dick had cooked for me, the tempting aromas having lured me early from my bed. The bacon was about half raw and the eggs pretty snotty, but I wasn't one to discourage people who wanted to work by criticizing their efforts. I ate the whole mess, assuring myself that a clean, lovely country like Montana couldn't possibly harbor nasty things like salmonella and trichinosis.

While I sipped the bitter coffee I was learning to like, Dick told me something of the history of the valley. There didn't seem to be any hard facts, though, and as an amateur historian I had little interest in mere legend and hearsay.

"There are old dumps all over the place," he said. "You might find some bottles and things, if you like antiques."

"I don't get it," I said. "Why would people come clear out here to dump their trash?"

"No, you don't understand. The stuff is at the old homesteads—you'll see them when you ramble around, after the snow goes off next spring. I used to hike all over the place, when I first started working here."

Dick didn't tell me why he had stopped and I didn't ask, preferring not to know if he had a bum ticker, and already caught up in the prospect of sifting through the residue of pioneer life. The artifacts a dump would yield were concrete evidence much more to my liking than some myth passed down through the generations, likely embroidered upon with each telling. Then it hit me that Dick was assuming I would stick around until spring came. No lack of self-esteem there! But then, what had I done to shake his confidence? Not one thing. *Tout au contraire.*

I glanced at him, and his face in repose seemed to have a rather mean cast. A real rough old ranny. I wondered if my fright of the night before had been misplaced, and if I actually had more to fear inside the cabin than out!

Sloughing off this disturbing idea, I pondered what Dick had said about old homesteads. Tales of the ancient Anasazi Indians of the Southwest shivered through my mind—a tribe that had abandoned their cliff dwellings long ago, for no discernible reason.

"Who were the people living here," I asked, "and why did they leave this lovely place?"

"They forgot to leave us a note," Dick said wryly. "After the snow melts I'll show you some of the old graves that aren't far from the road. Some are Indian with a circle of boulders, and a few have rocks piled up, like cairns. But the majority are just wooden crosses, with names and dates burned or gouged into them."

As Dick refilled our coffee cups, I tried to imagine this valley having been populated at an earlier time in history.

"Lots of the cabins were just trappers' digs," he went on, "but there were some families too. One place that burned down had a good foundation and a basement—lilac bushes and apple trees still grow there."

He got up and walked to the window.

"You can still see the ruts of wagon wheels where they came across the valley," he said, studying the vista of snowy meadow and mountains as though it were as new to him as to me. "In fact, there used to be an old thimble-skame wagon sitting at the edge of the pasture. It was in bad shape, and one wheel was missing. But when I came home from a . . . an overnight trip, it was gone. Someone came in and hauled it out of here."

"What a nerve," I said. "Did you tell anyone you were going to be gone?"

A harshness dulled his eyes as he said: "Yeah—yeah, I told a couple of people."

Someone who knew the combination to the padlock on the gate, I thought. Friend? Lady antique dealer, jealous of his all-night dates with another woman?

We sat in silence, Dick looking glum and I somewhat appalled at how I could build an entire scenario out of a few random statements. Yet it had the ring of truth, as my perceptions about things sometimes did. My mind's eye pictured covered wagons pulled laboriously across this valley by mule team or oxen, and I could almost feel the hopeful vibrations emanating from those long-ago pilgrims. Rousing myself with a shrug, I asked,

"What's this about Rowdy Joe Lowe being one of your ancestors?"

"Oh, you heard that?" he said. "Well, one of my sisters looked into it, but she couldn't find any proof that Joe had ever been married."

"Oh, but he was married to Rowdy Kate," I said, "and any man who bit off another's nose surely sired a few offspring here and there."

Dick gave me a quick suspicious look as though I'd caught him out somehow, but did not deny the kinship. His odd reaction, though, made me suspect it was just a rumor he had encouraged, to add to his charisma.

He began to tell me about different groups he had guided into the wilderness areas. As he talked, his voice flattened out and his face sagged into the downward lines of depression, whether at the contrast between those halcyon days and his present life, or some other worry, it was impossible to tell. I left him to his memories and spent the day getting my feet acquainted with a game trail that started behind the lodge and wound around the base of the mountain.

The hazy purple mist of twilight was filling the valley by the time I returned. On the drainboard lay two large trout, fairly begging to be cooked and eaten.

"What did you do, fish through the ice?" I said.

"Nope. Had them in a freezer, down at the lodge. They're just about defrosted—want to fry 'em up?"

"I'd rather just run them under the broiler," I said. "There's a lemon in the crisper, and . . ." my mouth began to water so copiously I could hardly speak, for I'd had nothing to eat since breakfast. Dick bowed to my culinary preference, and while the fish finished defrosting I made a spicy rice pilaf to go with them.

Dick seemed to enjoy our simple meal as much as I did, but after the table was cleared and the dishes washed, he surprised me by bringing out a bottle.

"But . . . but," I sputtered, "I thought you said . . ."

"Some people can't handle it," he said, "but I can."

I fervently hoped so, as he began to mix and toss down highballs at an alarming rate. After a couple of hours of steady imbibing he began to pound the table, muttering threats and curses, and naming several people against whom he apparently held a grudge.

There was a heavy iron bolt on the inside of my bedroom door, but I was fairly sure he could break it down with one lunge if he became really violent, which seemed increasingly likely.

"I believe I'll go to bed now, Dick," I said softly.

"No. Stay up and talk with me for a while," he protested.

"All right—just to the bathroom, then."

When I was in the bathroom he began a loud, petulant monologue, which he continued after I came out.

". . . and we were just little kids at the time, maybe seven and nine or thereabouts. Anyway, after the breakup the old man took us to Illinois on the train. There we were, all juiced up about the nice trip, and the bastard went off and left us there with his brother!"

Dick slammed his empty glass into the sink, where it shattered into ugly shards, and took a long gurgling swig right out of the bottle. I tried to make myself invisible, but his eyes, now mere slits gleaming malevolently, found mine and held me as though we were connected by a taut wire. When he spoke again, it was in a soft secretive voice more menacing than his bellows.

"One of my chores was to milk the cow. One night she stepped in the pail just as I finished, and got the milk full of cow dung. My uncle whipped me and then took me out into the woods and chained me to a tree, and set that pail of filthy milk beside me. 'Here,' he said, 'this is all you'll have to eat until you learn to milk a cow right!'"

I finally managed to tear my eyes away. Dropping my head into my hands, I silently mourned the maltreated little boy forever locked inside this angry man.

An ugly, grating laugh ripped out of Dick, and he added, "We ran away the same night he took the chain off—walked all the way back to Montana."

He put a clammy finger under my chin and raised my head.

"What do you think of that?" he snarled.

"I think . . . I think it's just awful," I stammered, closing my eyes against the grimace these painful memories had smeared across his face.

"Look at me," he commanded. "I went back," he said, his voice rich with some secret satisfaction. "Do you understand?"

I said yes, although I didn't . . . not yet.

Dick lurched toward his bed, still muttering, but the only word I could make out was "plowed."

Supposing that Dick would lie late abed, the next morning I slipped quietly out of the cabin.

The sky was cloudless, and so gradually that I was

hardly aware of its happening, a flush of pale pink replaced the luminous gray in the East. This in turn blended with a momentary suffusion of the most delicate ochre, and then all at once the sky was the clear stunning blue peculiar to Montana.

I had grabbed the key ring on the way out, and after some trail and error located the key that opened the back door of the lodge. The cavernous kitchen smelled faintly of oregano and sage, reminding me sharply that it was past breakfast time. A swift search revealed provisions left over from summer, and after cocoa and sesame crackers, I prowled at my leisure.

Dick had rushed me through too fast on the first tour, and this time I inspected everything thoroughly. I found high rubber boots in one of the closets, perfect for the trek I had in mind, and after stuffing the toes with tissue they fit well enough.

There was a master bedroom at one end of the building, and I sat for a while on the quilt-covered four poster. The canopied bed had a cave-like aura of security, and a feeling of contentment and continuity seemed to pervade the colorful room. There were half a dozen paintings, including two nudes—one a voluptuous red-head lying on her side with a marmalade cat perched on her hip; the other a brunette on her stomach, a black poodle stretched across her back like a popcorn-stitched sweater.

"Quite the bawdy boudoir," I murmured, "and definitely a happy place."

On my way out I spotted a down-filled jacket hanging on the back porch and slipped it on over my light coat. Dick had told me they left canned goods, blankets, and clothing on the unlocked porch in case lost hunters came upon the ranch when no one was around—which he claimed happened nearly every season. Some handy provisions might or might not keep them from breaking into the lodge.

I went back to the cabin, treading as lightly as I could, but a slight tinkle as I hung the keys back behind the door must have sounded like a rock concert to Dick's hung-over ears. He reared up and roared at me, "Take the survival vest if you go out of sight of the cabin. It's hanging in my bathroom."

I examined the garment, which I recognized as a fourteen-pocket Army field vest. This one was size XL, and the pockets were stuffed with items of value to a person lost in the woods; matches, compass, beef jerky, bandages, salt, and the like . . . all of which made it heavy as well as bulky.

"I won't need that," I assured myself, "just for a walk down the road."

Dick had gone back to sleep, and I put the vest in my closet so he would think I'd worn it . . . a thoughtless little ploy that was to cost me points down the line.

As I stepped outside again the sun crested the mountains, creating the dazzling illusion that the snowbank across the road was a heap of blazing diamonds. I started out at my usual brisk pace, reveling in the mountain air and stunning scenery, and after I had swung along for about a mile my peripheral vision was snagged by a blur of movement off the road.

Curiosity propelled me across the ditch and into the

woods. What had caught my attention proved to be a bobcat caught in a trap. There were streaks of blood on the snow, and I wondered if the serrated jaws had injured the cat, or if he'd been trying to chew his paw off to free himself, as some animals will do.

He hissed and spat fiercely as I approached, finally resigning himself to my intrusion with only an occasional contemptuous snarl. I had seen a lot of bobcats in the forest near my childhood home, but never at such close range. The watchful golden eyes looked oddly like buttons made by some meticulous craftsman, and for the first time in years I was touched with the desire to paint.

There was a soft thud behind me and I whirled around, expecting to find his mate leaping for my throat, but it was only a clump of snow that had slid off a pine bough as the sun warmed the trees. Then a slight tingling sensation down the back of one leg prompted me to turn back toward the cat. To my horror, I found that he had been able to drag the trap and himself just close enough to rip the back of my boot open from top to sole. My knees came unhinged and I sat down hard in the snow.

"You moron!" I berated myself.

The bobcat regarded me with dispassionate eyes, but I could have sworn his mouth curved up in a pleased feline grin.

"Out here a mile from home—why, if he'd slashed just a *fraction* of an inch deeper, you'd have lain here and bled or frozen to death!"

Struggling shakily to my feet, I returned to the cabin on trembling legs. One of those survival kit bandages would have come in handy to tie the gaping boot, which kept falling off. Lacking any other option, I broke off a vine and used it as cord.

My plan had been to sneak into my room and hide the boots, but Dick was already up and sitting at the table. There was a strange odor in the air, and he was eating a dish of glop that appeared on closer inspection to be fried brains.

"Where's that vest?" he barked.

"Oh, I only went a short ways," I said lamely.

"Don't matter! If you knew how many people have come to this ranch and never been seen or heard of again, you wouldn't be so bloody careless."

He paused to take a sip of coffee, and I backed toward my room.

"Here, hold it a minute. What's the matter with that boot?" he said. "Did you get tangled up in something?"

His eyes narrowed, and a frown creased his brow as he craned his neck forward and exclaimed,

"Say . . . that looks like the pair Missus Boss wears to go fishing!"

Any fool could see that push had come to shove.

"I'm sorry, Dick," I said. "I should have asked you if it was all right to borrow them, but I didn't want to . . ."

The sudden rage that flared in his eyes stopped my apology cold. I slumped down beside him, my snow-caked pants giving me a chill almost as frosty as the look on his face.

"I did wrong," I faltered miserably. "I *know* I did, but I never will again. I'll replace the boots when we go to town, and I'll never *ever* go fifty feet from the cabin again without the survival vest."

"Where is it—the vest? And look at me if you please, not at the floor."

"I . . . uh . . . I put it in my room."

An expression it hadn't been my misfortune to see before gradually developed on his face. If it's possible for cheeks to stiffen with indignation, his did. The frown deepened, his nostrils flared, and his lower lip jutted out in a savage pout.

"Out-and-out trickery!" he exploded. "Too dumb to wear it, and didn't even put it back. Trying to fool me!"

He smote his forehead as though it were all to much to bear, and then as though the blow had shattered his rage he said earnestly, "We can't have that kind of crap on a place like this, don't you see? We have to pull together, in trust and . . ."

Suddenly he reached down and yanked off the ruined boot.

"Now how on God's green earth could you have done that? Why, it looks deliberate to me."

I cringed, mentally preparing myself to be dumped back in Missoula. Just arrived, practically, and already I had proven to be a pain in the posterior.

"A bobcat did it," I said.

Incredulity bloomed in his eyes, and why not? It sounded like a bald-faced lie.

"Don't give me that kind of baloney," he said, the right side of his upper lip curling viciously. "Bobcats don't go anywhere near people if they can help it."

"Well, he *couldn't* help it," I said. "He was in a trap."

"A trap!" he screamed.

I hated to think what precipitous rise in blood pressure caused Dick's face to flame that awful shade of purplish scarlet. He hurried into his bathroom and the door of his medicine cabinet squeaked open. After the water stopped running I could hear him mumbling to himself,

"Blasted trespassers. Just no way to keep them out of here. Poachers, trappers, picnickers, antler-gatherers, hikers . . . you name it, we got it."

He came back and sat down, his fury under control, but enough of it leaking around the edges to keep me silent.

"Did you free it?" he said.

"What?"

"The kitty, did you let it out of the trap?"

I sighed. It had been a pretty bum day, all things considered, not at all what I had planned. I was tired, hungry, and uncomfortable, and feeling unfairly attacked from all quarters, or at least more viciously than my blundering warranted. Then without warning my temper blew. I stuck my nose an inch from his and yelled in his face, "Now you tell me how I could have done that!"

We glared at each other, two incompatible people apparently doomed to be forever plagued by misunderstandings. Dick shoved me away with a finger that felt like a rifle barrel in the middle of my chest.

"Even after what happened," he said coldly, "I don't believe you really understand how dangerous carelessness can be in a place like this. Well, you can horse around to your heart's content out there. I give up."

I hung my head like a rebuked schoolgirl, but Dick wasn't finished. Slow, icy, deadly, he doled out the hurtful words, building to a crescendo which I considered unduly histrionic.

". . . but the first time your reckless ways put *my* life in danger, you can snap your tack and GIT!"

"I'll go pack my bag," I said woodenly, starting for my room.

My silent dismay must have spoken to Dick on some level, for he stood up and said, "Oh, never mind."

Expelling a sigh, he went to the closet to get his cap and jacket.

"Come on," he said, "I'll show you how it's done."

"I'll have to change my pants and put on some shoes," I said. While I changed clothes, my mind kept fussing at me that he had called me dumb. Did I deserve that? Well, it was probably worth putting up with a little contumely to live in such a fantastic place. Yet I knew well that I had my limits. When I reached them, it would not be just a little steam-whistle toot like today's blowup.

We drove down the road to where the bobcat lay stoically licking its striped mustaches, hardly taking note of our arrival. Dick tramped around and located a forked stick which he held against the cat's throat until it was unconscious. Then he removed the trap and threw it into the truckbed. The cat regained its senses, shook its head, and limped away into the forest without a backward glance.

"A lesson there for him to pass on to his kittens," I said, "and a story for me to tell my grandchildren."

"You ought to write it all down for them," Dick said. "If they're anything like you, they'd probably get a big kick out of it all."

I vowed to keep a journal from that day on. There would be days when nothing happened, of course, but I could at least record the weather and temperatures.

On the way home, Dick reached over and patted my hand in a conciliatory gesture.

"Do you think we'll ever get along?" he asked sheepishly.

"I doubt it," I snapped, still smarting from the keelhauling he had given me, "but I intend to enjoy every last minute, right up until the whole shebang blows up in my face."

As it turned out there were very few days on which nothing happened, and if I'd thought I was there for a rest cure I was badly mistaken.

4
Elk Impersonation
and a Visitor

When I woke next morning, I lay wondering who could have set a trap so close to the cabin. Could those noises in the night be something other than wild animals? As far as I knew, Dick never locked the cabin door unless we were away.

That train of thought was soon derailed by another—what was it Dick had called one type of trespasser—antler-gatherers? Meaning that people collected the dropped horns to sell? I had heard they were prized as an aphrodisiac in some cultures.

"Maybe I'll pick some up myself," I thought. "A little extra cash is always welcome. After all, I can't stay here forever."

No, I couldn't stay forever, but I pushed away the pang of regret the knowledge of my eventual departure brought. There was no use mourning something that hadn't happened. I went into the kitchen to find that Dick had already left, and took my time preparing and eating hefty portions of bacon and hotcakes.

Since a hard-learned lesson is not soon forgotten, as soon as I was dressed I went into Dick's bathroom to get the survival vest. Glancing at the mundane items on the shelves of his medicine cabinet, I noticed a row of brown prescription medicine bottles behind some boxes of bandage on the top shelf. I moved the boxes and studied the labels on the bottles . . . Ornase, Lomotil, Elavil, Librium, Grifulvin . . . what were they all for? Feeling a vague uneasiness, I put things back the way I had found them. It was possible Dick was in poor health despite his robust appearance.

My ramblings that day took me far beyond ranch property and into the vast lonely reaches of the Lolo National Forest. When the sun was straight up I ate some cold rolled pancakes I had brought along and drank from an icy stream. Then I found a patch of bare ground the sun had warmed and stretched out to rest, listening to sounds around me and trying to identify each one.

The insistent knock of a woodpecker woke me. Soothed by the woodland lullaby of animal rustlings and wind in the treetops, I had slept deeply, but in the meantime a thick cloud cover had moved in. When I rose to start home I was totally disoriented and I realized it had been a mistake to guide myself by the sun instead of memorizing landmarks.

"The compass," I reminded myself. "That's why you're wearing this vest, remember?"

I took the compass from the top righthand pocket and then could not believe north was where the quivering arrow pointed. I started in the direction I felt was right, and finally came out into a clearing on a high ridge, from which vantage I could make out the lay of the land. Although the tributary leading to Gilbert Creek was dry, I could see patches of its sandy bed where the snow had been trampled or blown away. It took forty-five minutes of serious walking to reach it and then I kept the brushy banks in sight to guide me home.

My feet were tired and my load heavy, for I'd picked up two magnificent eight-point racks along the way. Over-confidence got the best of caution, and I took a shortcut across the left toe of Solomon Mountain, the only adverse result being that I overshot the ranch and had to backtrack.

Before long I cut onto a Forest Service road that made for easier going. It led right to our road and I was stepping along smartly, entertaining thoughts of a hot cup of coffee, when I heard a sound foreign to this isolated fastness—an engine laboring up the mountainside. It startled me so, I left the road and concealed myself in the brush, and while crouched there it came to me that female company might be on the way to visit Dick.

"And if that's the case," I warned myself, "I'd better not go home until after she leaves."

I knew that might mean a long cold night in the woods, so I was relieved to see a power company truck come into view, moving slowly on the icy rutted road. Giving in to another of my regrettable impulses, I held one elk-horn on each side of my head so they were visible above the bushes and wagged them around. The truck came to an abrupt skidding halt, and in the sudden pregnant silence I could no longer contain my good joke.

"Hi!" I cried, popping up from the underbrush.

The young man driving the truck exploded.

"You dumb broad!" he shouted. "What do you think you're doing?"

I stepped back a pace, my impish mood evaporating. After he finished mopping his face with a bandanna, he pointed a finger at me.

"Don't you *ever* pull a fool stunt like that again!" he roared. "People come up here all the time poaching deer out of season and . . ."

My expression must have shown that I thought he was overdoing it. A strange look flickered in his eyes for a moment and was gone, but suddenly I was positive he had almost shot me himself, and only jumping up when I did had saved my life.

"Come on, I'll give you a lift," he said. "I take it you're, ah, visiting Lowe, up here."

His rifle was lying across the seat when I opened the door, and with a quick slantwise look at me he shoved it back onto the rack.

"Came up to trim the branches growing into the power lines," he said. "A little prevention goes a long way, up here in the boonies."

He stopped once to use his chainsaw on a cracked limb that looked ready to crash down onto the wires. Then he lectured me some more about my folly, but when we approached the cabin he surprised me by saying,

"Maybe we'd better not tell Dick what you did."

"All right," I said, wondering why not. Did he figure Dick would put two and two together real fast? (Of course Dick heard about it anyway, via the mysterious mountain grapevine, and ever after greeted this fellow with: "Hello, Mister Almost-ladykiller.")

I made coffee and put out a plate of cookies, and as we sat around the table Dick regaled Danny with tales of our fictitious neighbor, "Bigfoot." Danny smiled indulgently until Dick said,

"Yep . . . why, this very morning I saw some of his tracks. Came out of the river and crossed the road, right down there below the cabin."

"You don't say," Danny said uncertainly. "Let's have a look."

He finished his coffee in one gulp and stood up, shrugging into his plaid mackinaw. My scalp began to crawl like a panful of rattlers when I saw the crystalline snow marred by large human-like footprints. Danny's freckles were dimmed by a sudden flush as he studied them.

"If we'd had a Chinook I'd say they were elk tracks, enlarged by the thaw," he said, a little tremor in his voice betraying his intense interest in the subject.

"Aw, come off it," Dick cried. "We haven't had a Chinook. And that doesn't look anything like elk tracks. What's the matter with you, Dan?"

He began to snort and paw his feet around in the snow as though he were an old bull elk himself, never letting up on the nagging.

"You're out in the woods just about every day. Tell me, did you ever see an elk with toes? I'll *swear*, I don't know why people can't accept a simple fact of nature without either going hysterical" (he stabbed a glance at me) "or making out that you're some kind of a nut for believing in such things."

We followed the tracks until they disappeared beneath the trees where no snow had collected, and then returned to the cabin. As he climbed into his truck, Danny responded at last to Dick's barrage.

"You'd better start coming to town more often. It's not good to sit around up here alone all winter like you do."

Both men looked at me, but I didn't feel it was my place to offer an explanation as to what I was doing there (if indeed there was one), and Dick only said,

"Don't look like much, but she can imitate a coyote so good you'd never know the difference. Just points her nose at the mood and lets 'er rip."

Danny goggled his eyes at me, speechless, and Dick added in a whisper, "She don't know what we're talking about. Pronounces it *ki*-yoat. Heeh! Yeah . . . well, so long, Dan."

I pretended not to have heard, but for a person with hyperacusis, a whisper is as loud as a shout.

The truck door slammed, sending echoes reverberating back and forth across the valley, and just so did Dick's unkind words bounce back and forth in my mind. I went directly to my bathroom and looked at myself in the mirror.

"It's true," I said. "You're a mess."

I hadn't been paying much attention to my hair, what with so many fascinating things to see and do. It hung below shoulder length and had taken on a ragged, bushy look. And when had I stopped wearing makeup? No trace of foundation, eyebrow pencil, lipstick—not even a touch of blusher. I started to put on some lipstick, found that the tube was used up, and tossed it into the trash.

Dick had hauled a cardboard box from under his bed and was rummaging around in it like a rat terrier in a hole.

"Read that!" he cried at length, triumphantly shoving a discolored and tattered newspaper clipping under my nose, "and *then* try to tell me there's no such thing as a Sasquatch."

I smoothed the fragile paper out carefully on the table and studied the photograph, knowing it was useless to try and convince Dick I kept an open mind about such things. The head of the Anthropology Department of a university in Idaho was measuring a track such as the ones we had just looked at, and the text below the picture quoted him as saying the footprints were spaced fifteen feet apart.

"Fifteen feet!" I cried. "Good grief—whatever the thing is, it must *jump* along like a kangaroo—not walk."

Dick gazed at me blandly, and the shiver that seemed to touch my shoulders with increasing frequency was joined by a slight stirring in my guts . . . an unsettling combination of excitement and panic.

Danny's advice apparently fermented in Dick's mind for a few days (uneventful days during which we sort of circled each other warily, like a couple of boxers, each reluctant to throw the first punch). Finally he told me it was time for a trip to town.

"Have to replace those boots you ruined getting too close to the bobcat," he reminded me, "and you should have a down jacket of your own. Clothes that are too big tend to get snagged on things and foul you up."

So I had found out, nearly hanging myself in the process.

"We'll pick up a few extra groceries while we're at it," he added. "Might get snowed in any day now."

"Snowed in?" I yelped. "You never told me we could get snowed in up here."

A dreadful look of impatience distorted Dick's features.

"Well, what would you expect?" he said. "In *November?*"

"I don't know . . ."

"At this altitude," he squalled, "this far north!"

I was sorry I had opened my mouth and managed to keep it firmly closed for almost an hour.

We stopped in Clinton to pick up the mail, and I posted a letter to each of my sons. These ambiguous missives had taken me a long time to compose, for it was hard to explain what I was doing on a ranch in the hinterlands of Montana as the season teetered on the verge of deep winter.

Dick came out of the Post Office with a stack of mail, which he proceeded to shuffle through. Then a couple of women popped out of the building and stood looking at us, and for an awful moment I thought one of them might be Dick's affianced, or even a wife who had slipped his mind.

"What's wrong with *them?*" I asked.

"I don't know," he said, glancing at the ladies before returning to his sorting. "Why don't you ask them?"

Not yet being accustomed to Dick's irony, I took him literally and rolled down the window.

"Is there something the matter?" I called.

One of them stepped back and the other forward. Although her chubby cheeks turned a mottled red, she stood her ground and said, "No mum. We ... just wanted to see what Mister Lowe's new woman looked like."

A car drove slowly past us, and a hatchet-faced matron stuck her head right out the window for a good gander. A few cusswords I hadn't used since third grade squeezed out past my clenched teeth. "Get me out of here," I choked. "Mister Lowe's new woman, is it? What did you tell them?"

"Not a thing," he said, "and I have to check and be sure all this mail is for the boss or us. Sometimes they put things in the wrong ..."

"Start this truck or I'll kill you," I hissed.

Dick sighed as though greatly put upon, started the engine, and drove us away from the inspection committee.

"Who were those fat women?" I asked.

"Oh, they're from up around Drummond someplace."

Handing me the mail to put in the glove compartment, he added: "What's eating you? You said you were raised on a farm. You ought to know what country people are like—curious as cats."

It was true. But I had been away from the country for a long time, and I had forgotten.

There was always something white peeping out of Dick's pocket, which I assumed was a handkerchief, so when he puffed up for a sneeze I yanked it out and held it under his nose. It was a plastic bag.

"What's this for?" I asked.

"Oh, that's just my barth bag," he said.

"Your *barth* bag," I affirmed, nodding while I ran down the list of "b" words in my vocabulary and came up zip. I had taken to sort of screwing up my forehead at Dick, rather than continually asking him what he meant. So I did my forehead thing, and he said,

"Sometimes I have a real sudden dizzy, sick spell. Don't want to splatter all over."

Not such hot news, considering that he was the one doing the driving on these treacherous roads, which surely required a clear head and full attention. I mulled the thing over and found it hard to believe that Dick, as a well-traveled man, would not know what they called those bags the airlines provided for queasy passengers. I fixed him with a relentless stare, but when he finally turned to look at me his eyes were innocent and there was not even the trace of a twitch around his mouth. Was he putting me on or was he not? Of the hundreds of times I had cause to wonder, I never knew for sure.

We arrived in Missoula and refreshed ourselves with coffee and doughnuts, and then did our shopping. As Dick stowed half a dozen bags of groceries on the floor of the truck's cab and the seat between us, I wondered why two people would require such an enormous amount of food. Then I recalled his outburst about being snowed in. It seemed a ridiculous idea, with the sun beaming benignly down from a clear sky, but I knew better than to say anything and get him started again.

Already I was longing for the clean peaceful silence of the mountains, but instead of heading for the highway Dick drove to an area of warehouses. When he parked behind one of the buildings, a stocky youth in striped bib overalls appeared in the doorway.

"Howdy Beartracks," he sang out. "How's it goin'?"

"Hi Scotty," Dick said. "Got some goodies for me today?"

Dick got out and sauntered to the door and they disappeared inside. When he returned he was carrying a bulging burlap bag. He tossed it into the truckbed, but I could smell it plainly. Fish. And a long ways from fresh.

Dick seemed in an unusually good humor on the way home. He even hummed softly, which I had never know him to do. For some perverse reason, his jolly mood aroused the opposite feeling in me. Those secretive ways of his . . . why couldn't he just *tell* me why he was hauling home a stinking load of overripe fish? Finally I said,

"That fish must be spoiled. Wasn't it under refrigeration?"

"Uh, no, it wasn't. Well, it's just heads and guts, actually."

"For crying out loud," I exclaimed, "if the owners of the ranch are so wealthy, why don't they just buy regular fertilizer?"

He hummed a little more, and then said, "Oh, rich folks like to save a buck if they can, just like the rest of us."

I saw that there was no use pursuing it.

A few minutes after I turned out my light and got into bed that night, I heard the sound of footsteps crunching in the snow outside. Sliding out of bed, I went to the window and peered out. Dick got the bag of fish entrails out of the truckbed, dragged it down to the lodge, and dumped the contents into an open trash barrel.

Pulling my wing chair over by the window, I made myself comfortable and settled down to watch. After about ten minutes a dark form lumbered out of the trees, and for one heart-quaking moment I though Bigfoot had come to call. Then the moon tore itself free of a clot of clouds and lighted the yard like a stage, and I saw that it was a brown bear.

"Bear confronts Beartracks," I said. "Well, I've always heard people do silly things when the moon is full."

The bear delved into the barrel and ate its fill, and then man and ursine seemed to conduct a fairly civilized conversation. As soon as Dick started back toward the cabin I dashed into the kitchen, to be in a position to start firing questions the moment he came through the door.

"Why isn't that bear hibernating?" I yapped.

"Oh, he will be," Dick said, showing no surprise at seeing me out of bed, fluttering around in my nightgown. "Any day now that old fellow will crawl into a hole someplace and have a good long snooze."

"Don't you know he'd as soon eat your arm as a fishhead?" I said.

It was clear that this had never occurred to Dick. He looked startled, and then a hurt expression softened his face.

"Why, he's a . . . almost like a pet."

"I hate bears," I snapped. "Back home, one of them came crashing through our kitchen window and scared the bejabers out of Mama. Wrecked the kitchen, and we had to go stay in the woodshed until Dad came in from the west 80 and shot it."

"Lots of bear around here, as you might expect," Dick said. "Want to play some checkers?"

"No. I'm going to sit up all night and see that the thing doesn't break my window and come into my room."

"Why should he?" Dick said. "He's well fed. Better get some rest—big day tomorrow."

I sat in my chair looking out the window, and before long the soft soughing of night-winds in the treetops had soothed my frets.

"Maybe I bit off more than I can chew," I confessed to the cold silent stars keeping vigil above me. "That man—that man is something else *entirely*."

I tried to think of anything that we had in common, but there didn't seem to be much outside of our mutual love of the wilderness. Of course, I didn't know Dick very well—and something told me I never would, no matter how long I stayed at Valley of the Moon Ranch.

Soon my eyes started slamming shut in spite of my efforts to maintain surveillance. I was forced to leave my lookout post and tumble into bed, and in the morning there was a bear doughnut right under my window.

As I was washing the breakfast dishes, Dick spoke to someone outside. We were expecting the propane truck, but I hadn't heard it drive in. A strange voice answered and I turned away from the sink as Dick came in, followed by an incredibly ragged and dirty person who carried his own ferally pungent atmosphere with him.

"Sit down," Dick said.

"Yes sir," the young man replied. He had a full beard and long stringy blond hair full of twigs and woodland duff, and his clothes hung in tatters on a body that seemed composed of sticks.

"This is Delbert," Dick announced, sitting across from him at the table. "Would you bring us some coffee please, and make him a sandwich?"

"Why sure—what kind would you like, Delbert? We have baked ham, some sharp Cheddar cheese, pastrami . . ."

Delbert, who had been gazing at me piteously, gave such a terrible groan that I thought he must be in extreme pain.

"Just anything, Jenny," Dick said, snapping his fingers. "Pronto . . . the boy's starving."

I stepped around smartly then. There was still half a pot of coffee plugged in, so I poured it first. Delbert drained his cup with three big slurps. I gave him a refill, and his eyes began to focus and take on a human aspect.

"Now," Dick said, "where did you say you started out walking from—Wisconsin, was it?"

Delbert nodded and suddenly flopped his head down on the table, falling to pieces as people are wont to do when salvation is finally at hand.

"All right, we'll talk after you eat," Dick said. "And in case you don't know where you are, this is Valley of the Moon Ranch. It's in Montana, between the Sapphire and John Long mountain ranges. You must have come through Butte, or close to it . . . did you?"

Delbert uttered a faint "uh" and turned his head over

so that he faced me instead of Dick, and Dick mumbled, "Sorry."

The boy's eyes followed my every move; he seemed to have trouble believing that this was an actual scenario and not just wishful thinking. At one point he yelled "Wah!" and his body jerked convulsively, and Dick's eyes stabbed at the pistol on the shelf. I hurried my efforts, wondering if food was going to turn this half-wild creature into a rational human being.

At last it was ready—a virtual Dagwood of ham, cheese, sliced tomatoes and red onion. I'd had breakfast an hour earlier, but my appetite came roaring back as I fixed our guest's sandwich. When I placed it before him he scarfed it down like an animal, and I had to force myself to stop gawking at him and return to the sink.

"Here! Not so fast," Dick said. "You'll get sick."

Delbert must have been a decent sort, for he saved a bit of crust, although we could see that it cost him dearly.

"For my friend," he said.

"Your friend?"

"Yeah, he's got a friend outside," Dick said. "Won't come in—gone woods-crazy."

Woods-crazy. A dark thrill coursed through me. I'd always known there was such a condition, and now here was a specimen I could study, right on the ranch . . . if I could catch him.

"I saw the shadow of a human the other day, up on the ridge," I said, "but I thought it was just a figment of my imagination."

Dick turned and gave me a quizzical stare.

"Is that so? Do you have these imagination . . . deals often, when you're out running around in the woods?"

The tone of Dick's voice irked me, but when my eyes met his the high glee in them melted me, as usual. Since Dick could no longer roam the wilderness, because of a tricky heart, as he put it, I knew it was frustration that caused him to needle me a bit now and then.

Delbert all but exploded with a big belch, and Dick turned back to him.

"You kids walked all the way here from Wisconsin?" he said.

"Yes sir, we did," replied the tattered hobo, "and it *never* went right, not from the very beginning. Connerd—he's only seventeen—he never did a blamed thing in his entire life 'sides work on that farm and jabber about going out West."

"What town are you from?" Dick asked. "Jenny here is from that neck of the woods."

"I'm from Luck," he said, grinning as though remembering the jokes doubtlessly cracked about the town's capricious name. He coughed, spat into his hand, and wiped it down one pantleg, which explained the odd stripes I'd been wondering about. "Yah, it's right close to the Minny-sodie border," he added although no one had told him that was where I hailed from. He clearly didn't give a rap about former neighbors, though, and in fact was staring mesmerized at the refrigerator.

"Shall I make a sandwich for . . . Conrad, is it? And would you care for another one?" I asked.

Would he ever. He gave out with another of those dying-cow moans, and Dick said: "Just make a bag of them, honey. You understand, Delbert, this isn't my place, so I can't ask you to stay."

"Oh sure," he said, jumping and looking toward the door, as though terrified that someone might force him to sleep inside a building. "Well, we hadn't hardly got a good start when some honyockers jumped us in the middle of the night. Scairt the . . . uh, scairt heck out of Connerd . . . tell the truth, he ain't never been quite right since. They took our whole outfit, everything but the duds on our backs, but Connerd, he wouldn't hear of going back home. Not as I blame him, you know."

Dick sighed and mumbled in my direction.

"Oh, go ahead and fry up those steaks . . . give them that bag of potatoes, too. I suppose we can go to town again in a few days."

"Thank you. You're very kind," I whispered, blotting my eyes with the dish towel.

"Say Delbert," he said, "I've got some old shirts and pants I was going to give to the thrift shop. You guys might as well have them, and what size shoes do you wear?"

My eyes swiveled at once to Delbert's feet. They were wrapped in burlap bagging, out of which oozed fresh blood. I was unable to repress a loud "boo-hoo-hoo," and Dick got up to drape a comforting arm across my shoulders.

"You fellows better head south as fast as you can leg it," he said. "Have yourself a hot shower first. Bathroom's to your right, and there's plenty bandages in the medicine cabinet. I'll put some clothes on that big chair for you."

Delbert stayed in there so long I though the shock of a bath had killed him, but finally he emerged in Dick's newest work pants and shirt. He had shaved off his beard and trimmed his hair to shoulder length. It gleamed like molten gold. Dick handed him a gunnysack filled with food and extra clothing.

"What else can we do for you, Delbert?" he asked.

"I'll never forget you, Mister Dick sir," the boy replied fervently. "I'd admire to have a little paper to stuff in the toes of these yere shoes, I see they's a bit long on me."

I though I saw a bit of green peeping out from between the pages of the newspaper Dick handed him. Then Delbert gave us a snappy salute and stepped out the door, hardly resembling the creature who had faltered in an hour earlier.

"Good luck to you boys," Dick called after him, but we never did get a glimpse of the elusive Conrad.

"He must be going to follow along, keeping to the woods, until they're out of sight of the cabin," I said. "Darn it, I've never seen anyone woods-crazy before, either."

"Maybe you have," Dick said, his stomach jiggling as he struggled to contain a belly laugh.

"You mean," I gasped, "Conrad is just a . . . well, a *figment*, like I was saying . . . and Delbert is the one who's woods-crazy?"

"That's the way I read it," Dick replied. "Got so tarnal lonesome he conjured up a friend for himself."

We pondered this idea for a moment, and then Dick chuckled softly and said,

"Free spirit, my kiester! That boy's a prisoner of Mother Nature, and she can be a mighty cruel, indifferent keeper at times."

We continued to gaze at the spot where Delbert had disappeared until Dick said,

"That shadow you saw flitting past . . . could it have been an elk?"

"Oh, I suppose so," I said, "or most anything. My eyes weren't exactly in focus at the time. I was quite . . . relaxed."

He gave me another of those unreadable looks.

"Hmm . . . my star boarder sits in the forest with her eyes out of focus and sees fignewtons . . . I mean figments. Don't that beat all?"

We went back into the cabin, and Dick prowled around for a while in preoccupied silence. Then he sat down, closed his eyes, and folded his arms across his chest. He held this Buddha-like pose for so long I began to wonder if he was still alive, and went over to peer at him. Only the rhythmic flutter of a vein in his neck gave evidence of life. Then his eyes flew open and he gazed at me steadily until I turned away and went into my room.

"All things come to him who waits," he called after me.

I pretended not to hear him. Maybe he was right, but the waiting was so delicious, and when it ended, what mystery would take its place?"

5
Mountain Music
and Montana Skeeters

The wisps of a dream trailed away as I woke—a happy dream involving a lake and a rowboat, with a warm breeze lazily turning the leaves of cottonwood trees. I turned over and stretched, sensed that I had been smiling in my sleep, and marveled at this glow of well-being.

My body was responding to the pure air and exercise, but there was something else. Was I energized by the emotion awakening within me? Was I ready for that? Could I stop it, or did I even want to? I only knew that I was beginning to like Dick much more than I had believed possible.

A voice whispered in my ear, "Maybe you'd better pull your picket pin and ride, before things get *really* complicated."

I didn't trust that voice. A lot of the mistakes in my life had been made because I'd listened to it. No, I would stand pat this time, try to work things out, instead of running away at the first sign of a ripple on the pond.

Dick was a slow starter. He grunted at me when I came into the kitchen and then continued to drink his coffee, gazing out the window as was his habit. Half an hour later he mashed out his cigarette and said,

"Guess we might as well take the trash to the dump today. We can put out a few bales of hay for the deer along the way."

"Feed the deer?" I said. "Never heard of such a thing—but then, I never lived on a play ranch before."

"They don't like it much," he said, "but they'll eat it when winter forage gets scarce . . . which it does, when the snow gets this deep."

We hoisted the trash cans into the Bronco and started out, picking up the hay from a barn at the edge of the meadow. The sky was clear, the air very crisp and cold, and the sweet fragrance of well-cured hay filled the vehicle as we slewed down the rutted, icy road.

"Something funny happened last night," I said.

"Yuh?"

"Just as I was going to sleep . . . sort of . . . sort of half way between awake and asleep, you know, I . . . no. No, I can't tell you. It's too silly."

"Come on," he said, "spit it out."

"Well, I heard music—beautiful music, like a symphony. Far-away sounding, but definitely music."

He didn't say anything, and I added,

"I know there's no radio reception up here. What do you think it was?"

"Mountain music."

"What's mountain music?"

Again Dick was silent for long moments. Then he shrugged and said, "Not everything in this world has a logical explanation, Jenny. Can't you just enjoy it, and let it go at that?"

A phenomenon. I reached over and patted Dick's arm.

"Thanks for taking me seriously," I said. "I was afraid you'd start teasing, but I had to tell someone, and you're . . . all there is."

"Yes I am," he said, giving me a quick sidelong glance, "and don't you ever forget it. Oh yes, my daughter Mary called last night, after you went to bed. She and the kids are coming for Thanksgiving."

"Oh, how nice," I said. "Shall we have a turkey then?"

"If you want to," he said. "Last year I just fried up some trout for them, but I know they'd appreciate a regular Thanksgiving dinner. Make out a list, and we'll get the stuff in Missoula tomorrow."

Dick nudged me and pointed to a long smear on the pristine flank of the mountain.

"Look, Delbert's tracks. See where he took off over Monkey Mountain?"

"Yes, but I see two lines," I said, peering past him. "Do you think we were wrong, that there was really a Conrad after all?"

"Naw. That second groove is where he dragged the gunnysack along beside him."

"Why do you suppose he didn't stay on the road?" I said.

"I have no idea, but I hope he doesn't steal one of the horses. I put them in winter pasture, right below where he looks to be headed. And what do you bet he'd take that big-barreled steeldust the boss likes to ride? Probably don't even know that horse thieves get hung out West here."

I started at his inscrutable profile and said, "Aw . . . you're funning me again, aren't you?"

"Nope. Of course, we don't print it in the newspapers or show it on television."

"This is like a different world," I mused. "You ought to secede from the Union."

"Wish we could. Close the borders, too."

"Why, then you'd never have met me."

"That's true . . . I take it all back."

We shared a smile, and then I said:

"Seriously, though, why do you suppose they hung all those horse thieves back in the old days? They had jails, didn't they?"

"A life for a life," Dick replied. "Putting a man afoot, back then, was about the same as killing him—except that it made for a harder death."

We reached the dump and set fire to our rubbish, Dick adding some brush so the flames leaped high in a cheerful blaze. While he tended the fire I poked through a nearby pile of older castoffs, hoping to find an old Mason jar or bottle that was still intact. Suddenly there was a boom behind me that made me jump.

"What was *that*? Someone hunting out of season?"

"Don't know," Dick said. "It sounded real close."

He walked a slow circle around the dump, peering into the trees and brush. Abruptly he bent down and picked up a twisted fragment of metal.

"Look here," he called. "This aerosol can blew up . . . I forget to tell you we separate the cans from the papers."

We considered this for awhile, and then Dick went over to the pile of cans and picked up a big mosquito repellent container. He tossed it into the fire, grinning like a friend, and then grabbed me by the arm and yanked me behind a big tamarack tree. In a few minutes there was another terrific blast and a projectile hurtled past us.

"I wonder why they all come in this direction?" I said.

"Well, there's plenty of cans. Let's try another one and see which way it goes."

That one, sad to say, went off prematurely and ripped a strip of flesh from Dick's right ear. The mishap didn't prevent us from spending most of the afternoon playing a sort of Russian roulette of the aerosol cans.

A light mist was invading the valley by the time we started home. Halfway there, Dick pulled to the side of the road and stopped the Bronco. He reached up to the rack behind us and took down a rifle.

"Good time to give you a shooting lesson," he said. "Still plenty of light, but there's no glare from the sun."

After checking the gun, Dick selected a target and fired. It seemed much quieter after the echoes had died away, as though the forest creatures had halted their activities to wonder at the boom.

"There's a handgun in the glove compartment," he said. "You can take a few potshots with that while I do some brush-up shooting. I like to keep in practice . . . no cops around here, so we have to defend ourselves in case of trouble."

I wondered if Delbert's stealthy arrival at the ranch had spooked Dick a little bit. The handgun proved to be an odd-looking blued piece with a vented rib along the top of the barrel. I wanted to ask Dick where he had gotten it, but decided I'd better not. It was loaded with six rounds, three of which I fired into an oval area of tree trunk scraped free of bark by some passing animal. The bullet holes, in an inverted triangle above the crescent-shaped crack, formed a "happy face" at which I stared until Dick took the gun and placed the high-powered rifle in my hands.

"Let's see you hit that," he said, pointing at a white rock across the gully. Never having been a top-notch shootist, I missed it by a foot or two. Rather than fight the big gun's recoil, I let it take me backward onto my seat, an awkward plopping-down that tickled Dick, but was probably less clumsy than lunging around trying to stay on my feet.

Dick seemed to relish his role of instructor so much I didn't have the heart to tell him I was already well versed in the use of firearms (farmers enjoy the occasional pheasant or rabbit too, and all they cost is a bullet). He picked the rifle up out of the snow, wiped it lovingly, and said,

"I got an elk with this gun, two years ago—had my own horse then—a bay with plenty of bottom. That's the color of hot blood, you know."

"Is it?" I said. "The only horse I had of my own was one of those pinto paddlers. They sort of throw their front feet out to the side . . . it's hard to describe."

"Yeah, I've seen them," Dick said, giving me a speculative look that made me wonder if the pinto had been an expensive or valuable horse. He tilted the rifle barrel and fired from the hip, and a vulture that had been wheeling lazily nearby came hurtling down, crashing onto the branches of a fir tree. My memory at once dredged up an image of a book Dad had often stuck his nose in to avoid my mother's anxious comments about our iffy future on the farm: *Plain Directions for Shooting on the Wing,* by An Old Gamekeeper, circa 1894. I wondered if Dick had read it, and then my thoughts swarmed back to my pinto so acutely that I could almost see the steam rising from her coat after a hard run on a frigid winter's day, smell it even—and the look in her soft eyes when I brought her a special treat . . .

"Her name was Ginger," I said. "A very gentle pony, with pretty markings and long legs."

"My bay wasn't long-legged," Dick said, gazing with blank eyes at the distant mountains. "Short coupling, powerful quarters, built for carrying a two-hundred pound man long distances."

I didn't comment, knowing that his mind was far away. He hadn't even noticed the blood dripping from his ear onto his shoulder.

"Not too good-natured, as horses go," he added, "and a wicked eye. Ever see a horse with a wicked eye?"

He turned and glared at me fiercely, apparently as an example of what he meant.

"Of course," I said, "lots of them." And people too, I felt like adding.

"Well, there was a horse of great endurance."

His voice fairly vibrated with yearning for the animal, but I didn't ask what had happened to it. Nor did I tell him of my Ginger's mundane ending, standing in the yard dying by inches of old age, simply lying down one day and never getting up again.

Glancing at Dick's still face, I suspected his longing was not only for the fractious bay horse, but for all the years frittered away—years that seemed to pass slowly, but in retrospect were hardly more than a lightning flash. My throat ached with compassion at what I read in his defeated stance, but I knew no words of comfort for a proud, independent man in his decline. Maybe he had wanted a place like Valley of the Moon to call his own, or even a more modest spread. We got back into the Bronco and drove home in a silence that seemed a fitting ending to our boisterous day.

We were late getting started to town next day, due to a rash of Murphy's-law type occurrences, and then we weren't halfway up the mountain when the truck's engine stalled. All Dick's fussing and coaxing did no good, and finally he sent me jogging back to get the Bronco. We towed the truck back to the garage, where he located and fixed the problem, and started out again.

It was one of those mercurial days, the likes of which lend validity to the old saw, "If you don't like the weather in Montana, stick around a minute!" There was a brief blizzard that forced us to pull off the road and wait when visibility reached zero. Then within moments the sun shone like a blinding disc in the impossibly wide blue sky, and the wind howled through Hellgate Canyon so fiercely the truck rocked like a boat.

It was mid-afternoon by the time we reached Missoula, and we were hungry for the lunch we had missed so we headed directly for the cafe by the motel.

"Hi, Binky," Dick said to the waitress as we walked in. It was the first time I had heard her name. While we were partaking of delicious chili I was overwhelmed with the incongruity of it all and whispered in Dick's ear, "I hate silly names like that."

Whispering is never a good idea, and I had no one but myself to blame for the ensuing ruckus. Paranoia started in her eyes and spread all over her face and body, and she watched us as closely as though we were a pair of stickup artists. While we were finishing our second cups of coffee she came over and stood by our table.

"Didn't know you two was friends," she said, fixing Dick with a hard look. "You didn't even say hello to her when she come in here the first time."

Dick was hard to flabbergast, but she seemed to have done the job. His eyes opened up like lenses snapping a picture—the fingers on both hands splayed wide. When he didn't reply, she shrugged and mumbled, "Guess I just don't understand people."

"I guess you don't," he said, recovering from his momentary paralysis. "Couldn't have been much plainer—we were total strangers, and I picked her up. Took her home with me that very night . . ."

She held up her hands, palms outward, as though to ward off more of what she obviously hadn't expected to hear.

"Seems as though you might have guessed," Dick went on, "since we left here together."

It sounded perfectly awful, and the old woman croaked out a low, long-drawn-out "Aaahhh . . . ," a keening moan like a premature dirge for all the lost sinners of the world. Clearing her throat viciously, she said in a hoarse whisper,

"Why no, I never drempt. I though she was a-gonna stay at the motel, and you just happened to walk out at the same time."

Binky's intense owlish eyes held us pinned in our chairs, and my face began to radiate heat. Noticing my flush, Dick said, "Bad as having Momma catch you out behind the barn playing doctor, isn't it?"

"I orter have known," Binky erupted, "what with your *reputation,* and the sneak-dog way you have of sidling up on a person's blind side and . . ."

She might have caviled all day (and I was all ears), but Dick interrupted her.

"Of course, we did the decent thing, you understand."

"What!" she cried. "You got hitched . . . *again?*"

"Why, no," Dick said, blinking rapidly. "What I meant was, we didn't sleep together until the following night—her idea, actually."

"Dick Lowe!" I screeched. "You tell her that's not true!"

He stood up and kicked his chair back. One leg fell off. The chair teetered for a moment and then crashed over. Tossing a bill on the table, Dick yanked me up by one arm and marched me out. I couldn't resist a backward glance, and the avid glint in Binky's eyes indicated that thirty years of serving people hadn't diminished her interest in their business one whit.

"What on earth got into you," I said, "saying a thing like that?"

"Oh, she got my goat," he said sourly. "Just because I've known her all my life, that doesn't give the old busybody the right to . . ."

"But people are probably talking about us already," I cut in, vexed by his careless attitude, or possibly at myself for getting into this crazy situation and not being able to walk away from it.

"Of course they are," he agreed. "That's human nature, and since we've got the name, we might as well have the game."

Well, there it was . . . tossed right out on the table. Already. I didn't speak until we were in the truck and under way.

"It would never work," I said.

"What would never work?" he asked innocently.

That set me back, but flustered though I was, I plowed on.

"We'd soon be at each other's throats, like you and what's-her-name . . . the last one you had up there."

I felt a bit of tension tingle between us, but he only said,

"We'll never know if we don't give it a try, will we?"

I allowed that to be the final word on the subject, but my mind continued to circle around it. It was beginning to seem that I was walking a tightrope in my efforts to remain at the ranch. And if we turned out to be as incompatible physically as we were just about every other way . . . forget it.

Our next stop was a department store, where Dick bought shirts and trousers exactly like his old ones.

Then he insisted on buying me something, so rather than make a scene I picked out some new jeans.

"No, now get yourself a coat or something," he blustered. "Here, how about this nice leather jacket? What if you had to go to a . . . a funeral or something, and you with nothing but a summer coat and a down jacket?"

There were strange rough undercurrents in Dick's voice. I met his eyes across the rack of coats, and saw that the giving of this gift meant something to him. There seemed nothing for it but to select a jacket in my size, so I did. He paid for it, and helped me slip out of my coat and into it.

As we walked toward the shoe store, Dick pointed out a skinny man standing on the sidewalk listening with a rapt expression to a buxom blond with an intricate beehive hairdo.

"That guy's a shirt-tail relation of mine," he said, "and the blond is his sister-in-law. Now watch this."

He introduced them and John, never once glancing away from the focus of his interest, asked Dick how the fishing was up his way. Without waiting for a reply, he enthused,

"Caught some trout up to Rock Creek last week, and you wouldn't *believe* the size of one of those suckers . . ."

As the man talked, I noticed that Dick was sidling around behind him. When John's hands swooped up to describe the remarkable length of his catch, Dick whispered something in his ear and gave him a shove.

"Pretty pretty pretty!" John cried, stumbling and breaking his fall by grabbing onto the nearest objects, which happened to be his sister-in-law's imposing breasts. Customers stared out of a restaurant window at the pair, laughing or frowning according to their interpretation of the scene. Dick was bent over, wheezing as he cracked up.

It seemed to drag on forever. John, helpless in the grip of some terrible compulsion, was unable to release his hold, and in fact began to knead the woman's bosom as she stood frozen with shock. I was just thinking I'd have to do something, when she brought up a huge black handbag and whacked him right in the face with it.

Dick managed to straighten up and propel me down the street.

"What did you whisper in his ear?" I asked.

"Oh, he's a mountain man too," Dick said. "More of a hermit type than I am, though. The poor slob sometimes doesn't see a female for months on end . . . always talking about how great she's built . . ."

"I don't need a three-page introduction," I said. "Just before you pushed him into her, what did you *say*?"

"Why, all I said was 'hain't they purty?'"

I considered the three words which, abetted by John's obviously ferverent fantasizing, had proved to be the catalyst resulting in one of those peccadilloes people seldom live down.

"Bet neither of them ever speaks to you again," I said thoughtfully, and wondered that no one had as yet murdered Tricky Dick.

He paused in the doorway of the shoe store, yelled "More of the same," and divested himself of each loafer with a vigorous kick. They sailed high into the air and the clerk reached up and caught them handily, which smooth choreography led me to believe this charade had been played out many times in the past. When the clerk placed them on the counter, I noticed for the first time that Dick's shoes were so old the many cracks caked with shoe polish made them look striped.

"You gave Delbert your best pair of shoes," I murmured.

Having earlier formed an opinion that Dick was a bit on the chintzy side—in fact, squeezed a nickel until the buffalo squealed—I was now forced to revise my thinking.

When we left the shoe store I expected that we would buy our groceries and then start home, but Dick drove to the edge of town and parked beside a tavern—The Big Sky Dive, according to a weathered wooden sign crookedly suspended from a rope on one side and a rusted chain on the other.

"Let's have a few drinks," he said. "Celebrate our . . . well, you know . . . meeting each other."

"All right," I said. "I could do with a Coca-Cola."

"Aw!" he exclaimed. "Want them to think you're a . . ."

"A *what?* Mary Poppins? I hardly think we need to worry about that."

"Well, at least have a beer to start out with," he coaxed.

He opened the door and we were hit by a blast of noise—strident music, people shouting and singing, glass breaking and chairs scraping—definitely unnerving when you've become accustomed to total quiet. We groped our way through the cigarette smoke to an unoccupied table.

After Dick left to get our drinks, I sat staring around at my surroundings, the likes of which I had never seen before in my life. The wall I faced was a thicket of deer and elk horns, and to my left a huge moosehead mounted above the bar glared down at the revelers with furious-looking false eyeballs. The longer I looked at that face the more it reminded me of someone I knew, so I turned to the long wall on my right.

The decor there was divided into roughly three sections, one of which sported metal street signs—Broadway, Orange, Howell, etc. The center portion had been plastered solid with old license plates representing every state of the Union, from the invention of the car right up to the present. The other section was hung with photographs of old-timers—mostly cowhands, with a few miners and loggers thrown in, and all engaged in dangerous-looking activities.

My eyes longed to close against this junk, but in the spirit of finishing a job begun, I turned and forced myself to examine the last wall. A round green neon sign, fat as an Outback snake, pulsed with the steady beat of an artery. The lettered part being entirely nonfunctional, I was unable to make out what it advertised. Around it was tacked a profusion of tiny tepees, miniature moccasins, and other cutesy-poo ethnic outrages. Already I felt queasy, and I hadn't even tasted my drink.

Dick was saying something about my gawking. I turned back to him and noticed that he had already finished his beer. Picking up my glass, I gazed into its depths, which seemed to be of a strange greenish-yellow hue—or maybe that was a reflection of the neon sign behind me. I hazarded a sip. It didn't taste like any beer I'd ever had, but putting up a game front, I persisted. Not having drunk a brew for a good long stretch, the effects were soon felt, and with the usual result—I got sleepy.

"Come on, let's dance," Dick said, trying I suppose to inject some liveliness into our drooping party. I don't know where he learned to dance, but his vapid shuffles in no way matched up with my energetic clodhopper style. We blundered across the floor, trying to get into step, and then I stomped on his worst corn. He bellowed like an outraged buffalo, piercing sound that cut through all the other racket and caused everyone in the place to turn and stare at us. Dick beat a fast retreat to the restroom, leaving me standing in the middle of the dance floor.

Before I could pick my way through the kickers and stompers to our table, someone gripped my shoulder and breathed into my ear,

"We don't waste wimmin in this country."

I turned to face a crudely handsome man in plaid snap-button shirt and Levi's, his corn-yellow hair hanging into his eyes from previous exertions. He began to spin me around, and from the odor of livestock emanating from his lanky person I deduced that his was an actual cowpoke and no cheap drugstore imitation. He whirled me energetically and sang along, only a little off-key, as the band played "Pins and Needles in My Heart."

Soon I was dizzy as a tick, and when the song ended I too headed for the facilities, where a raised threshold I had failed to notice tripped me up. I lunged across the room, arms cart-wheeling vainly for balance, and came a cropper against the far wall, rebounding to the floor where I lay palpating a growing lump on my forehead.

The sound of rushing water brought me out of my daze. A stall door scrawked open and a well-dressed matron proceeded across the room. She peered squint-eyed at the floor before placing each foot just so. Maybe she was afraid there were more bodies strewn around. Halted midway by some imagined barrier, she shoved at thin air, shards of light from her diamond rings skittering across the ceiling, and muttered ugly words about someone named Hankus.

"The walls are harder than normal here in Montana, aren't they," I remarked, releasing my throbbing head to prop myself on one elbow.

"Everything's harder here in Montana, greenhorn," she sneered, notwithstanding that I was dressed in jeans and my new fringed leather jacket, while she was tricked out like a New York model.

Eventually I made it back to our table, not at all improved by my little rest, and with a bad three-cornered rent in the elbow on my new coat. Right away Dick became terribly concerned that people would think he had put that egg on my face.

"She fell," he said wonderingly to the group at the next table, who were so far gone they wouldn't have noticed if I'd grown another head. "Yep, just stood there and fell down."

"No I didn't," I said crossly, "I was walking."

There was a persistent tickle of nausea at the back of my throat and every time I belched I tasted the chili.

"We better get out of here if we're going to get groceries," I said carefully . . . all those g's wanted to come out as d's.

"You don't like to go out and party," Dick cawed, as though it were a shameful flaw in my character. "Well, nobody's going to stop me from enjoying a few drinks with my friends now and then. I'll just have to go by myself."

"See if I give a crap in hell," I said loudly.

He narrowed his eyes at me.

"You were right," he said. "It's time to go."

As we were leaving, a double-braided Indian in a red windbreaker barged in, bumping Dick over against the doorframe.

"Watch your step, you pigsty paddy no-account," the man snarled.

"Big talk for a loudmouth Digger Snake," Dick responded, bringing up his fists. I scooted out the door, figuring myself in no condition to get caught in the middle of a barroom brawl, but they only pounded each other on the back.

"That must be how old friends greet one another," I thought, "here on the last frontier."

Since I liked to cook and Dick liked to eat, I suppose it was inevitable that he should gain weight. Still I felt responsible for his increasing corpulence and though if I could get him to exercise more he might burn off some excess pounds. One morning I asked him if he would like to come with me on my hike.

"I don't like to walk," he said, continuing to sharpen the elkhorn-handled knife in his hands. "Don't worry, this blubber will melt off fast enough once summer gets here and there's hard work to be done."

Mildly alarmed at how often we seemed to read each other's minds, I went outside and surveyed my kingdom. As I stood trying to decide which direction to start out in, Dick came out.

"Well, okay then," he said, "let's go up on that ridge across the road. Sometimes a herd of elk hangs around up there, when the snow gets real deep."

We trudged up the incline, and when we reached the top a half-dozen elk raced away, their light-colored rumps bobbing. Dick picked up a handful of Rocky Mountain olives and studied them.

"You know, Jenny," he said, "if you want to make a little extra money, there's an easier way than collecting antlers. You could make Montana skeeters—I saw some for sale a couple of years ago, at one of those tourist traps up by Glacier Park. I'll show you how."

As he walked around collecting the elk droppings, Dick accidentally dislodged a rock. We stood listening as it rolled down the mountainside, crashing through the brush. He worked an even bigger one out of the ground and shoved it over the edge. The earth trembled as it bounded along. At one point it smacked into a tree with a hollow thunking sound, and then blundered on its way.

"Here, let's try this monster," he said, happy as a kid at recess. We worked for a long time, sweating in the chill air, to free a great gray boulder from its bed in the soil. At last we got it positioned atop the ridge, pushed hard, and over it went. Listening in rapt silence, we followed its thunderous progress down the mountain. Then, from far below, came a horrible tinny crash.

"What was *that?*" I gasped.

"Omigod," Dick cried, scrambling backward down the slope like a big clumsy spider, "let it be my truck. Oh please Lord, let it be my truck."

But the Lord wasn't listening to Dick that day. We had kept the Bronco parked beside the cabin, behind Dick's truck, since the heavy snows began. There it sat, all bashed in, the boulder snugged into its side. We could not budge that rock, and I had to go around behind the cabin and have a laughing fit.

When I went inside, Dick was on the phone asking someone to bring a backhoe. He hung up and gazed at me, his face a study in abject self-loathing.

"How am I going to explain this to the boss?" he asked.

How indeed. It wouldn't be possible to conceal the evidence of our folly from a savvy insurance investigator. In the end, Dick paid the repair bill out of his own pocket, and we fell to fabricating Montana skeeters in hopes of plugging the gap it made in his bank account.

Breakfast was finished, the dishes washed and put away. On the table, spread out on sheets of old newspaper were the Rocky Mountain olives we had carefully dried and varnished. Beside them was a box of toothpicks, a pile of pipe-cleaners, and the grouse feathers I had gathered. Also close at hand were a small jar of white hobby paint and several fine sable brushes.

In the center of this assortment reposed an old felt hat, covered with porcupine quills donated by the fat old porky that roamed the meadow. It was used to the scent of humans, and Dick had walked right up to it and swatted it with the hat, whereupon it decided people weren't so great after all, and released a load of quills.

"Now then, watch closely," Dick said. "Three olives make up the head and body, and they're held together with toothpicks."

He demonstrated that step, and then poked four pipe-cleaners into the body, bending them to resemble mosquito legs.

"The porky quill is his stinger—see?" he said, warming to his work. "Be real careful when you handle those things."

He stuck a grouse feather into each side for the wings, and painted on a whimsical face.

"Why, that's cuter than a bug's buns," I said. "Didn't take long, either."

"Right. I figure we can sell them for about three bucks apiece next summer. Those tourists will buy anything. Give it a try why don't you?"

After a few attempts I got into the rhythm of it so that I could ruminate on other matters as I worked. I was feeling uneasy about tomorrow's Thanksgiving dinner, and especially meeting Dick's relatives.

"This daughter of yours," I said, "surely she isn't the child of that . . . umm . . . drunkard you were telling me about, is she?"

"No she isn't," he said shortly, "and I don't remember telling you anything—all I said was, I don't want any heavy drinkers around here."

"Owtch!" I yelled. I'd gotten a porcupine quill embedded in my finger and was trying to yank it out with my teeth.

"Don't do that," Dick said. "I'll go get the tweezer."

When we were settled again, I asked Dick if the woman was a native Montanan. He grew very quiet. His hands stopped pushing Rocky Mountain olives onto toothpicks, and his lips barely moved when he spoke.

"My oh my, the lady's mouth is unruly this morning, isn't it?"

It wasn't easy keeping that mouth shut, but I managed it, and was just congratulating myself on having sidestepped a nasty scene when Dick blurted,

"She was from down South. I thought she was a nice woman, but she wasn't."

"Oh," I said, very much regretting having opened this can of worms. I wondered how he had met a woman from so far away, but then he had met *me*, hadn't he?

"I think she had ulterior motives," Dick said, his mouth writhing as though the words took skin and all on their way out.

"She took out a big insurance policy on me. I believe she tried to poison me. Stop staring at me like that."

I looked down at my skeeters, which my clenching hands had reduced to dark rubble, and silently cursed myself for being a nosy shrew, for forcing Dick to disgorge these painful memories, for getting him started and now not knowing how to stop him.

"Say Dick," I said brightly, "You know, I've always wanted to tell you about that time when . . ."

"Shut up," he said. "We used to sleep in the big bed you're using now. She'd dirty all over and then flop her hands around—slapped a whole handful of it right in my face one night. I grew to despise her, but it was summer and the boss had to have a cook. It's almost impossible to find help in the middle of the season. You have to get it all lined up beforehand. So I was stuck with her. Talk about Hell on earth . . . I had to be on my guard every minute, hardly dared eat or sleep . . ."

I didn't realize I was crying until I noticed the puddle on the newspaper in front of me. Suddenly Dick jumped up and cried,

"God knows, it's a wonder I can even love another . . . I mean, *be with* another woman. How do I dare, really, after . . ."

But I had caught it. Oh yes, my ear had plucked from the ozone the word *love*, and now I hugged it close.

"Love another . . ." he had said. "Love another woman," he had been going to say. *Me?* It was a wonder he could love—could love me. He loved me.

My tears stopped as though a faucet had been turned off. Dick had swept all his cute little Montana skeeters onto the floor, but it didn't matter. Nothing mattered now but that Dick loved me, and I loved him.

6
The
Lowe Flyer

My subconscious must have worked like a trouper all night. It had lots of advice to hurl at me the moment I opened my eyes.

"You're still awfully naive about men."

Usually these admonitions came in my mother's voice, but this time dad's mellow baritone spieled out the lecture. "When Dick said *love*," it went on, "and quickly changed it to *be with*, he was referring to his other women friends—not you. And by the way, sprout, if you want to stay here so badly you'd better nail the relationship down to something a little more definite than friendship!"

There were a few moments in which to digest this, and then more brutal truths.

"If he'd used cruder language, you wouldn't be suffering all this starry-eyed confusion. But being a romantic, you read something into it that just wasn't there."

I wanted to shout *no* and argue the point, but the voice retreated, leaving me to ponder those unpalatable words. If all that were true, then the women Dick dated were indeed the ones he "loved."

It was hard to accept, but I had to admit my own experience pretty much bore it out—many men considered love and sex to be one and the same thing. Well, I would give the voice's counsel some thought, although it didn't really matter since I wasn't looking for another partner anyway. Of course, if one just happened to fall in my lap . . .

I stirred restlessly and swung my feet to the floor, which seemed colder than usual. Maybe I had taken Dick's words the wrong way, but this was Thanksgiving. I would count my blessings, instead of fretting over something every bet as unknowable as mountain music!

Snow eddied down in dime-sized flakes, and judging by the thick mantle of white on the mountains it had been falling most of the night. I showered and dressed in mocha wool pants and a silky blouse of robin's-egg blue. Then I went into the kitchen, moving quietly, for Dick was still asleep—flat on his back, his face pale and puffy-eyed. By the time I had the turkey ready for the oven he was up and sitting at the table, staring into his coffee cup. He couldn't even manage a grunt, and after awhile I said, "Are you all right?"

"Oh, sure. Had to take a sedative last night, and they take a long time to wear off."

My fault, I supposed, but I couldn't feel guilty about it. An unusually peaceful look on Dick's face told me that he had long needed to say the words I had dragged out of him.

He finally perked up when my apple pies filled the cabin with their delicious aroma of fruit and cinnamon. I had never seen Dick wear anything but the usual work clothes, but he shaved and dressed in some tan whipcord pants and a good-looking green and brown

Pendleton shirt. Onto his head, at a jaunty angle, he clapped a red billed cap that he sometimes wore. I'd always felt that his wearing of the red cap signaled a certain mood or occasion, but it could have been just coincidence.

"I've been thinking," he said, "that maybe we should drive down to the gate and meet them. Her van could skid off the road real easy . . . might be better to leave it down there."

"Okay," I said. "I'll leave the oven turned to the lowest setting and ride along. Won't it be fun to have some youngsters around?"

"They play outdoors mostly," he said, but there was a pleased look on his face. It occurred to me that he might be feeling nervous about this meeting too, and wondering how I'd take a houseful of children.

We got into the newly-repaired Bronco and drove slowly down to the gate, plowing as we went. A man with a similar rig was plowing between the gate and the highway.

"Our neighbor," Dick said. "He's been logging up by the border—home for the holidays, I guess, or maybe the snow's too deep now to log up there."

"Was it his wife who called the other day," I asked, "and told you some boys had climbed over the fence and were walking up our road?"

"Yep. They've been a big help to me, but I'm afraid they're losing the farm . . . taxes and such . . . even though she seems to work about eighteen hours a day."

Mary must have been parked on the other side, for as soon as the road was cleared a blue van drove across the bridge and stopped in front of our gate. Out of it piled three children and an attractive brunette in a black pantsuit and stylish red coat. She whisked a kiss across my cheek and said, "Dad didn't tell us he had company."

"This is Jenny," Dick said, and reeled off his grandchildren's names. We squeezed into the Bronco for the trip back over the mountain.

"They love to come up here," Mary said. "We don't come when the Finnegans are here, of course, but winter is really more fun in a way. Look, kids . . ." She pointed out three mule deer pogo-sticking their way up the side of Monkey Mountain.

Dick teased the children unmercifully, but they seemed to be old hands at giving as good as they got. There was a galvanized washtub leaning against the cabin, and as soon as we arrived the boys carried it to the riverbank, hopped in, and shoved off for a fast and furious ride that ended when the tub upset and dumped them out on the ice.

"You play right there," Dick called to them. "We don't need any lost kids around the place."

The shy little blond girl followed us inside, and I fixed her a cup of cocoa. While the rest of us drank coffee, Mary brought her father up to date on family doings. Then she excused herself to take a shower, explaining that the alarm hadn't gone off and they'd had to leave home in a rush to make it here by noon.

Dick had gone outside to lube the snowplow mechanism, and I was setting the table when a shrill scream from the bathroom ripped the air. Out burst Mary, buck naked and dripping wet, a cloud of dense white smoke billowing around her.

"Fire!" she shrieked. "The water heater blew up, and your house is on fire!"

Uttering a few screeches of my own, I tore outside to find Dick. He was not working on the Bronco, and when I went back inside I saw that the smoke was subsiding. A check around the water heater revealed no flames or charred places, but behind it was an object that resembled a huge, burned-out . . . *firecracker*?

I found Dick standing by his truck, mouth twitching, eyes dancing.

"All right. It was a smashing success," I said. "Now, how did you do it?"

"Do what?" he asked.

I studied the truck. There was a wire running from under the engine, and I followed it around the end of the cabin where it disappeared into a hole in the wall of my bathroom. Never one to let sleeping dogs lie, I went back to further interrogate Dick. "How did you set it off?" I asked.

"Just turned the ignition key," he said, a snort of laughter ripping out of him before he could get his mouth closed again.

"For crying out loud," I said, resisting the urge to strike myself in the forehead, "you had to drill through a foot of solid log to do it! All that work for a few minutes of chaos . . . makes me wonder what else you're up to while I'm out traipsing around."

Later on I began to suspect that the smoke bomb had actually been rigged for *my* benefit, and that Mary had unwittingly blundered into a trap set for me. I didn't figure that out until I was in bed that night, and was forced to bury my face in the pillow as my risibilities erupted in squeals of laughter at the thought of Dick waiting impatiently for me to take a shower. *And waiting.* We didn't tax the river for bath water, that was for certain. Dick purely hated to take a shower, and I, having been reared with the Saturday night bath in a tin washtub routine, would never be convinced that daily bathing was necessary or even healthy, and remained abundantly content with speedy little sponge baths in between the shocking drenchings.

I never did get to the bottom of that. When things calmed down we proceeded to eat ourselves into a stupor, and then played Aggravation until bedtime. Next morning I was wakened by a child's excited voice.

"Mama! Grandpa! Come see these great big *tracks!*"

I leaped from bed as though touched by a hot wire, and rushed outside to see what the granddaughter had found.

"Lookit here, Jenny," she said, pointing to footprints exactly like the ones Dick had shown Danny and me. I went back into the cabin, where Dick was looking out the window and groggily rubbing his eyes.

"Where's that tape measure?" I asked. "Oh, there it is on the dresser. Don't you boys want to look at the tracks?"

They shrugged and crawled back into their sleeping bags. Mary poked her head from under the covers of the spare bed, gave her father a long enigmatic look, and said to me, "I've seen those footprints before . . . lots of times."

Their lack of enthusiasm suggested there would be no discussion of the elusive Sasquatch. Still, I measured the tracks and made a notation of the sighting in my journal.

Several times that morning I tried to get Mary alone, to quiz her about various matters of interest to me. Dick thwarted my efforts every time, and finally I gave up. If I was to discover anything more about Dick's personal history, it looked as though I'd have to manage it by myself.

The weather was nothing less than perfect, and after we had eaten our fill of bacon and waffles we went sledding on Monkey Mountain. By the time Dick and I got our turn it was late afternoon, the slight thaw we'd had was freezing, and the road was slick as glass. I plopped down on his back and off we shot, before I even had a chance to get situated and find something to hang onto. His arms were so big and round in his sheepskin lined jacket I couldn't get my hands around them, and every time we hit a bump I bounced high into the air.

"Stop! Stop it!" I yelled, "I'm falling off!" But the wind whipped my words away before they were out of my mouth, and of course there are no brakes on a sled anyway.

The trees merged into a dark blur as we whizzed along, faster . . . *faster!* I held on to Dick's coat collar until it ripped off, and then grabbed his ears. He screeched like a gutshot panther, so I turned him loose and went back to practically free-floating above him.

Through frost-coated eyelashes I spied a curve ahead. My thought processes were as frozen as my nose, but my heart managed to quake "we'll never make it," and my guts pleaded "abandon ship now!" in no uncertain terms. But I was just a little too slow and into the bank we plowed, a blizzard of snow churning around us as we ricocheted across the road and hit a tree trunk with a THONK of skulls and the awful splintering crash of our wooden sled being almost mortally wounded.

I flew for several long-drawn out seconds, making an arc that suddenly dropped me with a splat and knocked the breath out of my lungs. Dick shoved off again, not seeming to notice that I was missing, and sped on for a few more yards. He missed the next curve and disappeared in the trees, and soon I heard his faint shout, "Okay . . . I'm okay."

My deflated lungs finally drew breath and I rolled over onto my back in the soft snow.

"Wow," I said. "Wowee . . . what kind of deal is *this?*"

Dick appeared, dragging the remains of the Lowe Flyer.

"Are you all right, Jenny?" he asked.

I nodded weakly, and he pulled me up and began to brush the snow off my clothes. I noticed that there were big ragged holes in both knees of his dress pants, and looked down at myself. There wasn't a button left on my blouse, and the cuffs of my pants were fringed as though done on purpose. When I took a step I discovered the entire sole of one boot was missing.

"We don't want Mary and the kids to know we spilled," he said morosely. You'd have thought falling off a sled was worse than disgracing yourself in public.

"Huh!" I said. "How do you intend to explain that?"

I pointed at the sled, which since the second mishap was minus the steering piece as well as one runner. We looked at each other.

"I'd better go find the rest of it," he said, but hoots and jeers from up the mountain informed us that the others had already seen evidence of our crackup. Dick spat over his shoulder, "It's all your fault, you know. You were a lousy co-pilot."

"Sure, Dick," I said. "Sure it is."

I think the closest I ever came to giving Dick an actual conniption fit was that day I came home toting a dead bald eagle in the bag which I now carried everywhere, in case of some stupendous find. I called him outside and dumped the carcass on the ground at his feet. The great eyes, fearsome even in death, stared up at us.

"Omigod!" he gasped. "Go put that right back where you got it. It's against the law to have one, or any part of one!"

While I gaped at him, he studied my face for any indications of wrong-doing. Then he sort of braced himself and said,

"Did you . . . you didn't *kill* it, did you?"

"Of course not," I said, "it was already dead—and what could I kill it with, anyway?"

I showed him the palms of my hands, which he examined as though they might contain clues of guilt, and then he knelt to look at the bird. There was no wound, as I already knew. He stood up and placed the eagle reverently in the bed of his truck.

"Come on," he said, "we'll drive as far as we can—get as close as possible to where you picked it up."

"It's not very close to the road," I said.

"Just come on," he said impatiently.

We proceeded to the spot where my footprints emerged from the forest, left the truck, and followed them back through the trees.

"Did you really walk this far?" he asked after a while.

"No, I flew, and walked back," I said.

He gave me a dirty look and I said to myself, if that old boy had any idea how far I *usually* walked, he wouldn't wonder why I need new boots so often.

Dick was panting heavily by the time we reached the place where the eagle had lain. I put it on the ground reluctantly.

"Couldn't I just have one of these nice feathers?" I asked.

"NO!"

"Well . . . *some* of them must die a natural death," I groused, miffed at being denied any kind of souvenir.

"That doesn't make one bit of difference," he said, and a cynical look flickered across his face. I knew he was thinking there were few natural deaths in this savage world of predator and prey, more violent in its way than the streets of big cities.

"Well then," I said as we drove back home, "in your opinion, what could have happened?"

"People run cattle over there in the wilderness area," he said thoughtfully. "Lease it from the government, I guess, and they put out poison for the coyotes. That eagle must have gotten into some poison, or maybe fed on the carcass of a coyote that died of it."

We rode on in silence for a time, and then I asked,

"Do any of the tribes still use those feathers in their head-dresses for their ceremonial dances and all?"

"Yes they do, but there aren't many eagles left. It's a big fine if you kill one."

"Should we tell someone about it?" I asked.

"I don't think so—and don't go back there. And *don't* pick up another one if you see one. Promise?"

"All right, Dick. I promise."

"Not so much as a claw."

"No . . . not even a claw," I said wistfully.

I did sneak back a few days later, though, carrying my sketch-pad and some charcoal pencils, determined to salvage something of the majestic eagle.

It was gone.

I stared around, unable to come up with any conceivable explanation for its disappearance. There were no tracks other than the ones Dick and I had made, and it had not snowed in the meantime.

Dick's trust meant a great deal to me, and already I was feeling badly about having violated it for the sake of sketching a dead bird's body. I stood pondering that, and gradually it came to me that there was an unusual dead silence in the forest, as though all its winged and four-legged inhabitants had either departed or ceased their activities. I glanced behind me, as though Dick had followed me here to observe my chicanery, and then I gazed up at the sky and around me at the great trees, and felt my various kinds of smallnesses more keenly than usual.

I started back in my footprints, knowing that after the soft sounds of my footfalls had faded, silence would continue to jealously guard this secret.

As Dick had told me, some mysteries must a mystery remain.

One morning I got up to find Dick already dressed and shaved and carefully brushing a new suede jacket.

"Oh, I didn't know we were going to town today," I said.

"Well, since you never like to leave the ranch," he said, "I wasn't even going to ask you to go along."

My mouth fell open. It was true that I detested going to town, but I'd never actually said so or refused to go.

After he left, I was puttering around the kitchen when a though sprang full-blown into my mind. "He's going to see someone . . . he is going to be with a woman."

After the first jolt subsided, I decided it didn't really matter. I had curbed my growing attraction to Dick when I perceived that he was unable to return it in kind, at least at this stage of his life. I didn't want to be hurt again, just when I could feel the wounds of a lifetime healing.

Curiosity, however, was a facet of my makeup not so easily controlled. Feeling rather mean and superfluous anyway, I decided to snoop. Walking over to Dick's bed, I yanked the cardboard box from under it. Whatever had previously stayed my hand during other opportunities to look in it had been rendered inoperative. I found that it contained nothing but newspaper clippings and two letters—one from his son overseas, and the other in the spidery hand-writing of an elderly person.

"Burned them all," I said, my voice acrid with disgust. "He must have planned this a long time ago."

No trickery, he had said . . . we must be able to trust each other, living in a place such as this. Dick's idea of trust apparently had nothing to do with what transpired between men and women. A blind spot? Or a code instilled in him by the father who had left his mother? Prickles like sudden heat rash ran along my arms and neck, and I kicked the box, sending it skittering back under the bed.

Common sense overruled my irksome feelings toward Dick before long. After all, I had no claim on him, and he was only behaving as any normal male would. His trip to town alone (by choice, as we both knew despite his excuses) had accomplished one thing, though—it catapulted me out of my dream world with a crash, exposing the reality of my life as though a lightning bolt had illuminated it. It was time to do some serious thinking.

As I sat at the kitchen table, doodling on a napkin, I realized that I had not truly contemplated the "big picture" of my life since my arrival at Valley of the Moon. I had, in fact, been lulled by its beauty into an almost somnolent state—a careless acceptance of my circumstances that might prove dangerous. I jumped up and went into my room, lifting my suitcase down from the closet shelf. Beneath its false bottom nestled my checkbook, and I scanned the balance with some satisfaction.

I hadn't been spending much money, and now I intended to become even tighter.

"Forewarned is as good as money in the bank," I said, slapping the checkbook against my thigh. "Obviously I can be replaced . . . this is not my home, and he is not my man. Well, I'll be ready to leave whenever I have to."

I wrote a check to the company I had called to pack and store the things in my apartment, and by the time I had finished addressing the envelope a familiar lifting of my spirits began. My mind toyed with the idea of a trip to Alaska when the weather broke.

I'd been a transient at heart since my teens, I suppose, when my parents left our home state. Being a minor, I'd had to go along and leave the friends I had gone to school with since kindergarten, to church with since my birth. That early uprooting had forever disabused me of the notion that there was anything permanent about a home. Why get settled when you'll only have to pack up and move someday? It was certainly nothing to get all bent out of shape about.

My husband had been the same way. He had great organizational abilities, and moving was one way he could use them. I hadn't been really surprised when he slipped out of double harness and started doing his moving around unencumbered by wife and children. The part I liked best about moving to a new place was decorating, so maybe a career as an interior decorator would have solved the problem . . . but how could I regard this very basic facet of my nature as a problem? I couldn't, and later in life I came around to suspecting that transience is an inborn trait, and not caused by some adolescent trauma as I had wished to believe. How else explain folks who live in the same spot for forty years but are *still* transients? (It takes one to know one.) Their bodies may be present, but where oh where have their minds and hearts flown off to? These armchair travelers study brochures, endlessly call airlines and trains for schedule information, make plans in minute detail, and stare at maps until they're cross-eyed.

It was well that Dick had his little fling when he did. In mid-December the weather abruptly turned to weird combination of cold and muggy, and huge, moisture-laden snowflakes began their relentless fall.

One section of the road had banks on both sides, leaving limited space in which to dispose of the snow turned aside by the plow. The storm let up for a few days, only to be followed by one of fiercer intensity and longer duration, and soon both sides of the truck were scraping on the way through the narrow place.

One day Dick did not return from plowing snow at the usual time, and after the early dark closed in I paced around nearly frantic with worry. I was just pulling on my boots to go look for him in the truck when I heard the sound of a faltering motor that I couldn't be sure was the Bronco. I stepped outside.

"What happened?" I called. "Why does that engine sound so funny?"

"Just overheated, I guess," he rasped through trembling lips. "Couldn't get through. We're snowed in."

Some vital spot inside my chest grew numb with shock for a moment and then began to scurry about, panicky as a mouse in a maze. *Don't fence me in*. He had told me it could happen, but I hadn't truly believed him.

Dick climbed stiffly out of the cab, his face a bleached-out oval in the light cast by the big bulb above the door. We went into the cabin, and he shucked his wet clothes while I started a pot of coffee. Then he pulled a chair up in front of the heater and sat in his bathrobe, his shaking hands tangled together as though trying to draw comfort from each other.

"Your hands aren't frozen, are they?" I asked sharply. "How did you get the Bronco turned around?"

He tried to light a cigarette and dropped it.

"Had to back it a long ways," he said. "Nearly all the way to the barn. Wasted time trying to dig a turn-around with the shovel. Couldn't make a dent in that stuff."

He shivered and drew the chair closer to the heater.

"No, I don't think anything's frozen. I'm too tired to eat right now—just bring me some of that coffee when it's ready."

"You'd better call someone with a Cat to come up and knock some of that snow out," I said, "while the telephone lines are still up."

Dick shook his head, his jaw jutting out in defiance.

"There'll be a Chinook in January," he said. "There always is. We'll just wait it out."

My mind flew to the canned goods in the cupboards, upon which my hearty if not downright prodigious appetite had made deep inroads. Would there be enough? I though of the crops my parents had lost to hail, flood, late and early freezes, drought, all the while trying to predict the weather. In my experience, making plans dependent upon what the weather was going to do was nothing but a fool's game, but there had been a stubborn finality to Dick's words so I kept my own counsel.

"I did everything in my power to keep that road open," he said.

"Of course you did," I assured him. "Everything humanly possible."

There had been a tremor in his voice, and I finally understood that it was pride that prevented Dick from calling for help. He might even have made a bet with one of his cronies that he could keep the road open this year. Well, pride and vanity had been the downfall of legions since history began, and I could only hope that Dick's attitude would not result in a tragedy at Valley of the Moon Ranch.

The days of deep winter drifted quietly by. When nights were clear the stars glittered with incredible brilliance above us, but more and more night-time became a long gray muzzy interlude, cozy in a somehow dangerous way, as the snow fell and fell as though it would never stop.

Dick seemed to drift into a fatalistic acceptance of our plight, but I could not sit for hours staring into my past, as I was sure he was doing. There was a pair of snowshoes hanging in the garage, and as the snowpack deepened I made my expeditions on them, ranging across the white expanse of the valley and up into the foothills. I ate like a starved wolf after these treks, and apparently Dick ate out of boredom, for every time I looked at him he was nibbling. The lower our food supply dwindled the more we ate, as though engaged in a macabre contest to see who would be better equipped against the starvation to come.

When we were down to a few eggs and a dozen cans of food, I realized it was up to me to get help. Dick would not, or could not, make that call. I waited until he was down at the garage puttering around, and then picked up the phone with some vague idea of asking the Forest Service to send a Caterpillar up. Dick would be furious, and no doubt I would be on the road again when it became passable, but at least I would be alive. When I put the receiver to my ear, though, I discovered with a heart-jolting wrench that the line was dead.

Gilbert Creek was our water supply, and one day it froze so deeply the pump quit—something Dick claimed had never happened before. I hauled jugs of water from Spooky Springs on the Lowe Flyer, which was serviceable after a make-do repair job.

On days when the temperature fell to such outrageous lows that I feared part of my anatomy would freeze if I ventured out, I stayed inside and sketched pastel scenes from the window with chalks I had bought after the gorgeous bobcat renewed my interest in art. One scene in particular turned out well—the silver-gray luminous frozen river with snow-covered meadow beyond, and in the distance the dark spires of fir trees and the mountains rearing up like misshapen birthday cakes dribbling bands of frosting down their sides.

"That's a nice one, honey," Dick said, peering over my shoulder as I initialed the picture and dusted off the excess chalk. "Could we have it framed for Mary's Christmas present? Of course, she won't get it in time . . ."

"I'd be proud to have someone hang it up," I said. "Plenty of others, too. Maybe your granddaughter would like that one of the squirrel eating out of my bird feeder."

I looked up at Dick for confirmation, but he was gazing out at the mountains.

"Ever notice," he said, "how different they look on a cloudy day?" He glanced down at my picture. "You did the top part when the sun was out—caught the way it makes the mountains blaze like jewels with that new coat of snow."

"Yes, I filled in the rest after the clouds moved in," I said. "Do you realize it's been snowing every night?"

"Yep. Must have added three or four inches just the past couple of days."

Dick turned from the window, his face slack with apathy, and I felt a rush of pity. It hurt to watch the aging of this man who had been hunter, range rider, breaker of wild broncs . . . who had, in short, actually lived the life of the Westerner which had now become legendary, and a source of fascination for people the world over.

"Could I get you something to read from the lodge library?" I asked, putting away paper and chalks.

"No, I've read all those books already. Did you bring up the rest of the food from their pantry?"

"Yes, I got what was left of it yesterday. There were just some cans of grapefruit juice, gelatin, and a couple of bags of potato chips."

"Well, at least it's sustenance," he sighed. "I've got a bone-deep feeling this will be the worst winter in fifty years or more."

His face brightened a little and he added,

"I may have to take a buck, if we don't get a break in the weather soon . . . wouldn't be the first time I lived on meat straight, either."

"Aww . . . wouldn't you get in trouble?" I said. "People can't just hunt whenever they want to, without a license or anything, can they?"

Dick's expression remained serious, but his eyes were lit from behind with a flame of rascality.

"Who's to know?"

7
Snowed In

Unless there was an actual white-out blizzard, I usually hiked around on snowshoes everyday. But I'd been sick with a cold, so it was a total surprise when I opened the door one morning to find snow packed against it clear to the top. I must have screamed, for Dick tore out of his bathroom, long-john trapdoor flapping behind him.

"A winter straight from Hades," he said, eyeing the marble-like slab. "Hope the propane holds out."

He threw his weight against the barrier and didn't make a dent, and when I poked a finger at it, it felt like rock.

"You don't suppose it goes clear across the road to the bank?" I faltered, a ripple of alarm stirring in my solar plexus.

"No doubt about it," Dick said soberly, "and we don't have a shovel in here . . . not that a shovel is any good against a wall of ice. Well, a person can't think of everything . . . and whoever heard of shoveling your way *out* of the house?"

I had, but I didn't say so. Suddenly I wanted some fresh air, and right now. I rushed into my bathroom, pushed aside the curtain, and slid open my window.

More snow. At the very top was a space of about three inches, and by hauling the clothes hamper under the window and standing on it, I was able to get my nose up to it. After dragging in several gulps of fresh air I steadied down and felt my heartbeat return to normal.

There was no use even checking the other windows. They all opened outward, so even a foot or two of snow above the sill would prevent them from opening. Trying not to dwell on the fact that we were not only imprisoned on the ranch but in the cabin, I went back into the kitchen. Dick was busily kneading a gluey white mass on the cutting board, his arms and shirt-front coated with flour.

"I don't know what you're gonna do," he announced, "but I'm going to make bread."

"Why, we don't have all the ingredients," I said, amazed at the idea.

"Maybe I know some old Indian tricks," he said.

Maybe he did. His face held no clues. Although a white man, Dick had been reared on the Flathead Reservation, and for all I knew might have a whole bag of Indian tricks.

"Guess I'll clean up the house a little," I said without much enthusiasm.

"Good deal," Dick said. "We're getting to be a pretty stinky outfit since our water supply failed."

I got a pan and knife, and began to shave snow from the bank against the door. After a half-hour of hard labor, I put my gleaning on the stove to melt.

"Toss some of your dirty clothes out here," I said. "I'm going to hand-wash a few things."

While the snow was melting I defrosted and wiped out the empty refrigerator. There was a wilted bell pepper behind the crisper, and I was about to toss it into the garbage when Dick yelled:

"Give me that! Hot dog, I can cook up a pot of chili."

"Looks about half rotten to me," I said.

"No, a soak in cold water will bring it back to life." So saying, he got a bowl and helped himself to part of my hard-won wash water and immersed the pepper in it.

Then he tore around searching the cupboards, muttering and banging the doors, and producing only a dented can of tomato sauce and a bottle of chili pepper.

"I thought we had some dried onion flakes left," he said.

"No. I used them up and threw the jar away."

Then nothing would do but that he search our copious garbage, making a terrible mess on the floor around the cans. Finally he shouted "eureka" and held up the container, which did have a few bits of minced onion still clinging to the sides. I didn't see that it added up to chili, however.

"You have to have beans," I said. "Chili is made with either meat or beans or both."

He sat down to think this over, and after a while a delighted expression settled over his features.

"You know," he said, "I just remembered why we had this big bottle of chili pepper. They had a Mexican cook once, back when I first started working here. The boss said no matter what they told her, she pretended not to understand and cooked up a big pot of beans every other day. They got so sick and tired of beans, he brought the bag in here and hid it."

Dick jumped up and flared his nostrils in every direction, like an animal locating something by scent.

"Let's see . . . I know they're not in your room, because the Mex was living in there at the time. It seems like he was fiddling around here by the door . . . well, you've got better ESP than I do, Jenny. Get it in gear."

I walked over to the door. ESP, as he called it, was not something that came like a dog when you whistled. It seemed more a matter of elimination anyhow, so I began by feeling every inch of the door-frame. Dick bounced with excitement behind me but I took my time. Then I went over it again pressing and then knocking.

I repeated the whole procedure on the logs around the door-frame, and when I got to the knocking stage one spot yielded a hollow sound. There were tiny cracks in all the right places.

"There's your hidey-hole," I said.

Dick whipped a knife from his pocket, inserted the blade in one of the cracks, and pried gently. Out popped a section of log, about six by eight inches, and in the niche was a large plastic bag of pinto beans. It had been opened and taped shut again, but only a small amount of beans had been used. Dick let out a whoop, his eyes glowing like embers. I hadn't seen him so happy since he set off the bomb in the bathroom.

I stuck my hand in the hole, but there was no gold, no fat roll of greenbacks, no heap of gleaming gems. For that matter, considering the fix we were in, the food had more value to us than any amount of money we couldn't get out to spend.

The odors filling the cabin all morning were tantalizing, and I was practically drooling by the time we sat down to lunch. His bread had flopped, but the chili Dick dished up looked like prize-winning stuff. I chewed up a big mouthful, and it was undeniably delicious. But when I swallowed, something *dreadful* began to happen to my throat—flames were searing all the way from epiglottis to stomach. I rushed to the water jug, using two glassfuls of the precious liquid before I could even breathe again. It all seemed to stream back out of my eyes and nose, and I began to cough.

Dick gazed out the window, ignoring my agony as he continued to eat. He ate my portion too, and then had the effrontery to finish the whole pot, while dark suspicions multiplied like bacteria in my mind. When I could speak again, I said,

"That's the last time you ever get to dish up the food."

"And why is that, dear one?"

"You know very well why! You dumped extra chili powder in mine so I wouldn't want seconds, and you could have more for yourself. I hope you get a bad bellyache."

"Why no you don't. We have no working toilets."

"You . . . are . . . incorrigible!" I choked

There was still a kernel of doubt, though. Maybe Dick actually *did* have a cast-iron gastro-intestinal tract. He rubbed his stomach, expelled air from both ends, and said softly, but not softly enough,

"What price entertainment?"
And then I was sure. Hurrahed again.

It was hard to stay angry at Dick. He had smoked his last cigarette long ago, and must have been suffering. Still, he didn't complain as he humbly harvested butts from the five fragrant trash cans lined up in a row awaiting a trip to the dump. He retrieved all the small nuggets of tobacco nestling next to the filters of these butts, which were soggy with various rancid liquids and flavored with specks of God alone knew what.

He rolled these nasty snippets into newspaper, and when he had smoked the last of the horrid little teasers he took to pacing up and down the cabin, stomping to one end, whipping around, stomping back.

Survival instincts I didn't know I possessed flooded my brain and body as I observed this man who looked long over-due to blow. Fight or flight, they insisted—but there was no way out of the cabin, and Dick outweighed me by close to a hundred pounds. What was I to do in the event he actually went berserk? Another unwelcome notion crept into my mind . . . maybe Dick was claustrophobic, and his distress was more deep-seated than the nicotine withdrawal, which would ease eventually.

I went into my room to lie down and think about it, although a nap was out of the question while he was making the cabin tremble with his thunderous footfalls. As I lay striving to come up with some way to cope with a raging, insane Dick, my gaze lingered on the ceiling, which a former tenant had festooned with dried flowers, herbs, and vines. Certain of the leaves had a vaguely familiar shape, in fact, I could have sworn I'd seen a picture of one vine just days ago. I sat up and started to leaf through the top magazine of a stack on my bedstand, and there it was—*kinni-kinnick*—a weed smoked by the Indians, according to the article accompanying the photograph.

Well! So. He wasn't the only one with a few old Indian tricks.

What with all this mental activity going on, I hadn't noticed how quiet the place had become. I went into the kitchen and found the "cigarette paper" strips Dick had cut out of old newspaper. He was on his bed asleep, his face looking tortured even in repose.

After hauling a chair under the *kinni-kinnick* hanging from my ceiling, I yanked it down and spread it out on the kitchen table. I stripped the leaves from the vines and ran the rolling pin over them a few times, soon achieving a pile of what anyone could see would make a fine tobacco substitute. No doubt it would have been even better if I had washed off the dust and cobwebs, with their desiccated flies still entangled, but at that point there was no time for niceties. I got the jar of white glue down from the shelf and went to work and was just pasting the seam on the third and last of the lumpy objects when Dick woke up.

"What are you doing, Jenny?" he asked sleepily, looking over my shoulder.

"I made you some smokes," I said proudly.

"Is that so?"

His voice had a hopeful note, even in the face of the crudities on the table. He picked one up and smelled the end of it, and about half the contents ran out, cascading off his chin and onto his chest, where they disappeared in the V above his first shirt button.

"Hmmm," he said, not willing to examine this gift horse too closely. "Seems like I did this once when I was a kid, and got sick—corn tassel, or some such crap."

He took a kitchen match from his pocket, scratched it on his pants, and lit one of them, almost setting his sideburns afire as the excess paper flared up. He took a tentative puff.

"Oh that is bloody *awful!*" he wailed. "That's so terrible, it's in a class all by itself."

He paused and made a move as though to squash it in an ashtray, but something stronger than willpower drew it straight back to his mouth. He gave me a woebegone look which suggested he might as well get this over with, and took another drag—a deep one this time. The clock hadn't ticked three times before he turned sort of green and streaked for his bathroom like a hosed cat. Maybe he couldn't walk, but he sure could run. A big blat of laughter broke out of me, which I tried to disguise as a coughing fit. Teach him to doctor my chili.

After awhile Dick came slowly out of the bathroom and picked up the rest of the cigarettes. He crushed all of them between the palms of his hands, grinding fiercely. He threw the remains all over the floor and stomped them so viciously you'd have thought he was killing snakes. Then he said,

"You know, sweetness, I've been wondering if I hadn't ought to quit smoking. This just might be a good time to do it."

There wasn't much else he could do.

You might imagine New Year's would be just another day in our frozen world, but thanks to the resourcefulness of my cabin-mate, it turned out to be quite a . . . blast.

While sweeping Dick's bathroom, I noticed a bucket of brownish water with a repulsive-looking lump in the bottom of it. He was sitting in his chair reading and glanced up just as I kicked aside the bread-board which, since the chances of doing any baking were nil, had been pressed into service as a cover for the hole he had hacked in the floor. Before I could dump the contents of the bucket, Dick screamed "NO!" so loudly that I almost dropped it, and rushed over to grab it from my hands. He clasped it to his breast like a favored child that I had tried to paddle.

"What is the stuff, then?" I asked.

"Oh, it's just . . . well, it's a piece of plug tobacco I found behind my bed. Thought I'd soften it up a little, and have a chaw."

"So, you give up smoking and start chewing," I mumbled. Something didn't sound quite right. Why would it take half a gallon of our limited water supply to soften a small hunk of dried tobacco?

Things got stranger and stranger. Next day, which was December thirtieth, Dick came into my room before I was up and stood staring at the dried plants adorning the ceiling.

"Good Lord, you're not going to make any more of the *kinni-kinnick* cigarettes, are you?" I asked.

"No, no . . . but we're in luck. There are two or three good-sized clumps of mountain sage up there."

He yanked them down, and by the time I got out of bed they were boiling in the bucket of brown water the tobacco had steeped in. I made no comment, but such a pungent odor was beginning to fill the cabin (which smelt plenty gamy to begin with) that I had to stick my nose into the space at the top of my bathroom window for a few minutes.

About mid-afternoon, Dick dumped a can of cayenne pepper into the pail, stirred it vigorously, and set it on the drainboard to cool.

"Dick, what on *earth* are you doing?" I asked.

"Aw, it was supposed to be a surprise," he said, "but it's hard to keep a secret in two rooms. I'm making tanglefoot for our New Year's Eve celebration, and wait 'til you see what I've got stashed away."

I doubted he could hide anything I couldn't find, but I was wrong. He kicked aside a throw rug beside his bed, yanked up a floorboard, and produced a bottle about one-third full of whiskey.

"What tremendous willpower you have!" I cried.

"Yep. Many times I wanted a snort *bad*, and especially having no smokes."

He poured the concoction from the bucket carefully into the bottle, shook it up, and placed it in the center of the table.

"Be perfect by tomorrow night," he said proudly. He stepped back, regarded his handiwork, and added, "All it lacks is a snake-head for that extra little tang."

We whiled away December thirty-first playing hot games of checkers, interspersed with periods of re-reading old periodicals to calm down. My luck was running hog-wild that day, and after I beat Dick three times in a row he jumped up, dumped the board, and bellowed like an enraged bull. Unfortunately one of the black checkers was lost forever, and according to Dick, to use a substitute was to invite the direst kind of bad luck—not only at checkers, but in every area of life. (Such are the notions entertained by those who dwell too long on mountain-tops.)

When Dick recovered from his snit he entertained me with more stories of pranks he had pulled on "dudes" he packed into the wilderness areas (some of them pure fiction, I was sure—sort of a combination of hindsight and wishful thinking). Then we sat in companionable silence and watched the short winter day darken gradually into the deep black of a cold cloudy night.

After our New Year's Eve supper of canned spinach and potato chips, I was hit with an overwhelming sleepy spell. When you are hungry a good deal of the time, food tends to have that affect. But since it was my first New Year's at the ranch I was determined to stay up and usher it in, so I started jogging around the cabin to keep myself awake. When Dick saw me leaning against the sink, asleep on my feet, he got two highball glasses out of the cupboard and announced,

"Okay, it's time to start the festivities."

After pouring several inches of the murky fluid from the whiskey bottle into each glass, he drank a few swallows from one of them. His expression didn't change, but his complexion took on a radiant wild-rose hue.

"Great balls of *fire*," he croaked, "that stuff's got a kick like a Georgia mule!"

He cleared his throat noisily, and beads of sweat began to break out on his forehead. He felt his jaw and then his nose.

"I don't feel like myself," he said, "but then I don't feel like anybody else, either."

He cut his eyes slyly up at me and added,

"Aren't you going to drink yours? Come on, honey-bunch. Be sociable."

Feeling cornered, I picked up my glass. As soon as it was near my nose I got a whiff of a really ghastly stench, and hastily put it down. I looked carefully in the bottom of the bottle for snake-heads, fish-heads, worms—it smelled like all three.

"Killjoy," Dick sneered. "Party-pooper."

I marched to the cupboard and got down the one remaining can of grapefruit juice. I opened it and poured into my glass an amount equal to the hooch, fig-uring it was acidic enough to disable if not kill most of the germs. I hazarded a nip.

It had a quite indescribable taste, and yet I can't say it was *bad*, exactly. No, on second thought, not bad at all. I took a slightly larger sip. It warmed my mouth, teeth, tongue, throat, and the cockles of my heart.

I hadn't touched whiskey since I was sixteen and some of my classmates dared me to drink down a half-pint. It had darned near stopped my clock.

"But this isn't really whiskey," I assured myself. The undeniable truth of the words overruled my caution, and I drank down a good slug.

"Not bad after the first few swallows, is it?" Dick asked, his voice seeming to issue from somewhere beneath the floor.

As he refilled his glass I stared at his mouth, which had puckered and wrinkled up like a hundred-year-old toothless crone's. Wondering if the stuff had done that to me too, I rose to go have a look and went reeling sideways. My head struck the log wall with a hollow boom.

"How did you do *that?*" Dick exclaimed. "The THONK from your skull, and the one from the log, were in perfect harmony. Best mountain music I ever heard."

"You're already inebriated," I said stiffly, proceeding into my bathroom. As I examined my lips, I could hear Dick laughing.

"Well, I'm glad he's having a good time," I muttered at the bleary-eyed woman in the mirror. "I'm beginning to feel sicker."

By the time I got back to the kitchen, Dick had left off snickering and was once again feeling his face.

"Yes, your head's still there," I said, "Even if you can't locate it with both hands."

There was now a large ugly pistol lying on the table. Some ancient warning of my father's, regarding liquor and firearms, tried to force its way up from the bottom of my brain. Dick spoke, derailing the tenuous thought before it could complete its trip.

"I always shoot into the wall exactly at midnight on New Year's Eve," he said. "See those holes over there? One for each year."

I wasn't paying any attention, figuring it to be just more drunken blab and concentrating on not losing my supper since food had become such a scarce commodity. The clock read ten minutes to twelve, and I was thankful that I could soon go to bed.

Some time later I was gazing at the cookie jar on the shelf and had an almost hallucinatory revelation that there was one last chocolate chip cookie in it, which we both had overlooked. The cookie jar was shaped like a squirrel, and I knew for a fact that the large tail was hollow. In my besotted cleverness, that was where I was sure the last cookie nestled unnoticed.

I got up and took a step toward it, and a split-second after something hot fanned past my nose, I heard the BLAM! of the gun.

"Oh God!" Dick screamed. "Darling, I almost shot you!"

I wouldn't have teased him if I'd noticed he was going completely to pieces.

"That was pretty drastic," I said. "I know you're sick and tired of me, but you could have just told me to stay in my room."

There was a moment of dead silence. Then the gun still wavering in Dick's hand hit the floor with a thump, and he gave several short barking coughs as the acrid fumes of gunsmoke swirled toward the ceiling. Suddenly he took me in his arms, moaning like a wounded animal, his body shaking from head to foot.

"I think we'd better call it a day," I said, disengaging myself from his strangling embrace and wishing heartily that I'd retired hours ago and hang the celebration.

"Happy New Year, Dick, and many more."

He followed me into my bedroom and stood beside my bed, trying to unbutton his shirt.

"Why, what . . . what are *you* doing?" I squawked. "You told me you'd never sleep in the same bed with anyone again, after that . . . ah . . . nasty business with your last wife."

"I lied," he said, yanking the curtains shut against those thousand eyes the night is reputed to have. He crawled into my bed, shoes and all, and peered up at me like a naughty boy.

Oh my. What a contretemps . . . if I refused, I'd probably be sent packing when the thaw arrived. On the other hand, if I gave in and became just another of his women, wouldn't the result be the same before long?

I opened the drapes and looked to the heavens for counsel, and in a few minutes there was some deep breathing from the bed. Dick had either passed out or gone to sleep. Suddenly I was no longer sleepy. The cayenne pepper had percolated into every nook and cranny in my body, and was raging around like hellfire. After mussing up the covers on the empty side of the bed, I punched a dent into the pillow where my head would have rested.

If he woke up figuring he'd done something he couldn't remember, so much the better. *I'd* never tell, and butts to buttons he'd never ask.

I eased into the wing chair and sat grinning into the darkness until the blackness outside my window shaded into a soft flannel-gray, and then got up to begin a new year in the Valley of the Moon.

8
The Chinook Cometh

One morning I woke to such an unfamiliar sound, I wasn't sure but that I had passed on to another world.

Drip. Drop. Drippity-drop.

I sat up suddenly. The *Chinook?*

Leaping out of bed, I rushed into the kitchen and yanked open the door. The bank of snow was completely gone—vanished overnight! Well, I couldn't be sure of that, since we hadn't opened the door for some time—preferring to ignore the stuff that held us captive in order to concentrate on thinking up ways to annoy one another (surely one of the last stages of cabin fever before homicide).

I dashed to the sink and turned on a faucet, and a blast of air and frigid water shot out. Opening the kitchen window, I heard the faint steady *chug chug* of the pump as it brought water into the pipes. In the milk-gray light of dawn I saw that the river had broken up into a jumble of ragged hunks of ice, which were rearing up and colliding with each other as they moved downstream.

"Dick, get up!" I yelled. "Look outside . . . we're free!"

Opening his eyes, he muttered "Chinook." Then he rolled over toward me and said "false Spring."

Before he was even out of bed I began to burble in his face about the wonder of it.

"Wonderful, sure," he said, "but it won't last."

He sat on the edge of his bed, scowling out at the cerulean sky as though it were some freak of nature.

"We're going to have to tow my truck over to the other side of the mountain and leave it there," he said. "Just drive the Bronco between here and the gate."

Seeing my amazed look, he added, "Should have done that a couple of months ago."

"But . . . but surely," I stammered, "we won't be snowed in again . . . not *this* year!"

"Not only possible but very likely," he said. "It's too dangerous driving my truck on this road in the middle of winter. You can tow me over in the Bronco, and . . ."

"Are you serious!" I cried. "Why, you've never let me drive it more than a mile before. If we really have to do it, why don't *you* tow *me?*"

"*Because,*" he gritted, clenching his fists, "the truck has to be steered just right or it'll slide off the cliff and pull the Bronco along with it. You don't know how."

That was for certain, and I didn't want to learn. Maybe Dick did not place a high value on his own life, but every moment was precious to me, and I resented his asking me to take this risk which seemed so unnecessary.

Taking my silence for acquiescence, he got up and ran some water in his sink. It must have already been lukewarm, for he hopped into the shower, humming a cheerful ditty as though going to almost certain death were the most ordinary thing in the world.

When he came back out, I was still standing by his bed, trying not to think about the impossible thing he was insisting I do. He sat down and began to do a meticulous manicure on his fingernails. Good grief! Could this dude possibly be my old bunkie? He started on his feet, blithely chopping off months of accumulated corn, callus, and other horny excrescences, and using up half a jar of medicated foot cream.

"Have you started the coffee?" he asked, an edge of annoyance sharpening his voice, but a growing sense of foreboding held me rooted to the spot. Finally I tore myself away and dressed hastily, wondering if this long, cooped-up isolation had affected either or both of us mentally, and to what degree. Danny's voice replayed chilling words in my mind: "Better come to town more often."

When I came out of my room, Dick was brushing a red plaid jacket I had never seen him wear.

"Sorta like trying to force a shotgun shell into a .22," he grunted, stuffing himself into it. It wouldn't button across his stomach, but he wore it anyway, and his red cap. Uh-oh! He may as well have waved a red flag at me. All this, just to drive his truck down to the gate?

When he had the cap arranged at the proper angle he marched to the door, darting a hopeful glance at the stove in case a pot of coffee had miraculously materialized there. He held the door open after he went out, and I like a mesmerized fool walked through it and got into the Bronco. Since I seemed to have about as much future as a cow in the slaughter-pen anyway, I might as well die trying to haul Dick and his half-ton truck across the mountain.

I warmed up the Bronco. I did not care for engines, motors, or machinery of any kind, and I did not like to drive.

Meanwhile, Dick hitched the tow-chain and spieled out last-minute instructions, which I ignored—they weren't going to do me one bit of good when the crunch came. My agitation must have gotten to Dick at some level, for his voice began to waver uncertainly. "Now, don't . . . uh . . . don't let it get too slack, so it jerks, you know, when you . . ."

"Shut up," I hissed, "and get your butt in that truck if you're coming with me!"

As soon as he got one foot in the truck I stepped on the gas and went roaring down the road. He blared the horn at me, but I knew if I stopped I would never start again. I speeded up, hit the brakes, and then floored it again, giving him a terrific jerk. The chain didn't break but the honking ceased, and seconds later there was an explosive crash and the raw sound of ripping metal. A glance in the rear-view mirror told the tale—he hadn't gotten the door closed before my abrupt departure, and it had slammed into a tree and torn off.

When we got around the first bend, the sight that met my eyes shivered me from brainpan to tailbone. The Chinook had only affected lower elevations, and instead of a bare road, I was faced with dangerously glittering ice and treacherous half-rotten snow. *Pull the Bronco along after it . . .* we had hardly gotten a good start up the first hill before the wheels were up to the hubs in slush, and when we reached the next switch-back I could see deep drifts of snow flung across the top of the mountain like tired, soiled clouds resting there.

I tightened up, my bad vibrations tainting the atmosphere. Now I would pay with my life's blood for getting myself into this alien icy world where roads hung precariously off the sides of mountains. The worst place looked like about a forty-five degree grade with a corkscrew in the middle. Too slow and I wouldn't make the grade; too fast and I couldn't make the turn.

"Walk the tightrope, idiot," I husked out of a mouth gone dry as stale crackers. One of the front chains tore loose and began to bang and flop around, the racket adding to the nightmarish aspect of the drive. Abruptly my reasoning abilities, and then my mind itself, were shut down by the instinct for survival that comes raging into play when all else has failed. Glaring at the road out of eyes that had forgotten how to blink, I went at it.

With incredible luck and wrenching effort I managed to get past the worst turn, and was about to congratulate myself when the engine faltered and died. Fumbling with the key, I distinctly felt the right rear wheel of Dick's truck slip off the edge of the road. The gully was practically bottomless at that point, and I was helpless to blot out a vision of the Bronco sliding after the truck, exactly as I had been warned, crashing onto it when both vehicles hit bottom, mashing Dick to a pulp, and hurling me into the roof with skull-splitting force. This gruesome preview inspired me to claw at the emergency brake, but my sweat-slick hands couldn't grasp it.

Then both the truck's right wheels were over the cliff, the Bronco inching inexorably backward after it.

My breath was coming in big gagging wheezes by the time the stalled engine roared to life. I gave it a little gas and the wheels spun; after an agonizing eternity they gained purchase and slowly, ever so slowly, the Bronco eased back onto the roadbed. Soon the truck was in place behind it. We crawled to the crest in sickening anticlimax and rode our brakes down the other side. When I stopped, the truck plowed into the rear end of the Bronco, sending it crashing into the gate. The chain links caved in like paper links on a Christmas tree, and one of the posts snapped off.

"His legs must be about as noodly as mine," I groaned, for once having no desire to giggle in the face of misfortune, "or maybe he burned out his brakes. Oh well . . . we'll just have to step up our production of Montana Skeeters to pay for all the repairs."

I got out of the Bronco and staggered back to the truck, trying hard to ignore a growing certainty that Dick and I were one of those bad combinations that attract disaster, which seemed always to be trailing in our wake.

Dick stood beside the nearly total wreck of the truck he loved, ghastly pale, and stiff as a toy soldier. Only his hands twitched and jumped, like small caged animals wild to be free. I looked at them, hiccoughing softly from time to time. Dick gazed at something beyond my left shoulder. After awhile he sprang into action, as though his hard thoughts about the debacle had distilled it into something potent that lent him a maniacal strength. He shoved the ruined gate open, pushed the truck through the gate. Then he motioned for me to join him, and wired the gate shut behind me.

"We aren't . . . are we going to town in the truck, with no door on the driver's side?" I quavered.

He gave me a look that shut me right up, and said "We sure are" in a voice that made me think the truck wasn't the only thing that had gone over the edge that day. We drove to Missoula in silence, and Dick stopped in front of the market.

"Stock up on groceries," he said, fumbling a fifty-dollar bill out of his wallet. "There are some things I have to do. I'll call you in a few days, and you can come pick me up."

He stalked off down the street, and after he was out of earshot I said, "Ask me no questions, and I'll tell you no lies."

Having no intention of driving back to the ranch in a vehicle sans door, I made all haste to the body shop which had repaired the Bronco after its unfortunate run-in with the rock. The mechanic's eyes opened wide as they took in the truck's crumpled front end and the gaping rectangle where a door should have been. "That's not Beartracks Lowe's truck, is it? Shoot!" he exclaimed. "What happened?"

"I'm not sure," I said. "Could I get a loaner while you fix it? I have to get back to the ranch."

The manager came out of his office and provided me with a nearly new Ford truck boasting automatic transmission, a radio, and other niceties Dick's no-frills rig lacked—trusting of them, all things considered. But then, they were probably well insured. "The Bronco will be in again next week," I said.

They both stared at me as though I'd just pulled the pin on a hand grenade, and I hopped into the loaner truck before anyone could have second thoughts.

"I don't suppose you know what happened to it, either," the mechanic called after me.

I shook my head and twittered my fingers at them. Finding reverse, I backed out and drove away in my cherry-red prize. When I glanced back they had come outside and were watching my progress down the street, both pairs of lips going lickety-split. My stomach mumbled, reminding me that I'd had no breakfast, let alone lunch. When I walked into my favorite cafe, Binky's expression told me that she knew very well I had not washed my face that morning nor combed my hair nor given any attention to my teeth. While I wolfed down pancakes and sausage, she stood beside me wordlessly examining the filthy jeans I had jumped into in my rush to get dressed. I considered explaining that our laundry facilities had been nonexistent for weeks, but figuring that would result in a tit-for-tat unexpurgated unloading of her troubles onto me (and I was sure she had plenty of them), I avoided the subject. She turned away and began to mutter, and it seemed I would have to listen to her complaints after all—or perhaps she was only talking to herself.

"That man—nothing but a double-dealing polecat. Soon as something else catches his attention, you'll be out of there so fast . . ."

A bunch of young rowdies came in shoving each other around and trying to shock people by talking dirty, and all at once I was pierced with longing to be back at the ranch. My head was throbbing from city air, and in case I failed to mention it, Missoula is one of those places which smell exceedingly strange at times.

I hurriedly gathered as much food as I figured I could pay for at the grocery, then I headed for the tules, listening as I drove to the mellow ballads of George and Hank and all those wonderful artists. Yes, a fine thing, radio reception, but I wouldn't trade it for the mystery-freighted silence of Valley of the Moon—not if you threw in a million bucks to boot.

The next song, "Bluebird Island," brought warm memories that occupied me until I turned off the freeway and had to give my full attention to the road and weather, neither of which was ideal. The damaged gate almost proved to be my undoing. Dick, in his burst of hysteria, had wired it so tightly that blood was streaming from my fingers by the time I got it unfastened and dragged open. After driving the truck through and transferring the groceries to the Bronco, I was trembling with exhaustion. I maneuvered the Bronco until I could use it to push the gate shut, since both were already half shot anyway.

I drove the rest of the way like an automaton, skidding over sheets of ice and spraying slush six feet into the air, and by the time I reached the cabin my face was burning and my head seemed to be floating somewhere near the top of the cab. I stuck the perishables in the refrigerator and left the rest to put away later. Then I tended to my lacerated hands, swallowed two aspirin tablets, and fell into bed.

It was late afternoon when I woke, feeling lethargic, but my temperature was back to normal. After eating some toast and soup, I remained at the table writing up the day's events in my journal. After I had finished that my thoughts turned to Dick, and I wondered what urgent business had sent him helling off down the street on foot. Leaving the table, I curled up in his easy chair, which contained faint traces of the smell of gasoline and motor oil from his clothing, as well as other unidentifiable masculine odors. His absence from the cabin left a gap in my reality which I seemed powerless to fill.

"What makes Dick tick?" I said into the silence. There was a "whuff" outside the kitchen window, as though in answer to my query, and I hurried to close it. I had left an open jar of honey on the drainboard.

"Careless of me," I chastised myself. "Bears can probably smell honey from a mile away."

My long nap had put me off schedule, and bedtime came and went. Midnight found me back in Dick's chair, absorbed in a paperback book I had picked up at the market. A part of my mind monitored the night sounds outside without interfering with my concentration, until something crashed into the wall. Then I dropped the book and leaped up with a breathless involuntary shriek.

"Must be a Sasquatch," I muttered, pressing one ear anxiously against the door. "That darned Dick left a tire-iron leaning against the cabin, and now Bigfoot's trying to pry the door open with it!"

It sounded too much like the dialogue of a low-budget science fiction movie, so I left off and listened as the noise began to travel up the driveway and back down again with a metallic clanging racket that chilled my blood. However, it also tortured my bump of curiosity. I got Dick's .38 Police Special from the shelf, took it off safety and cocked it, and switched on the outside light. Then I yanked the door open.

A battered bucket moved slowly along, propelled by little black legs. Behind it trailed a fluffy pale tail.

"A skunk," I gasped. "And the poor devil's caught in the handle. Shoo . . . get away from here!"

He continued his rambling, ignoring me, and I knew I'd have to take action if there was to be any sleep that night. His lack of fear was encouraging—no fright, no spray, right?

I put the gun away and went back out, grabbing the pail with one hand and the handle with the other. I yanked hard, the bale came off the bucket, and the skunk shot out. I almost made it back inside before he got into firing position and let me have it with the only weapon at his command.

And yes, we had no tomato juice.

After I had showered and added the skunk event to the already lengthy day's entry in my journal, it occurred to me that the skunk is not an animal endowed with enough curiosity to venture into a bucket for no good reason. Meaning that . . . the pail had been rigged and baited? When and with what?

There was only one possible explanation. Dick had been up and about long before I woke, and had been playing possum when I came out to tell him about the Chinook. I tried to recollect what food had been left before I bought groceries.

"Two cans of beans and a can of mackerel," I mused, "and they're still in the cupboard."

Did Dick have a secret stash of food somewhere? Living here among wild creatures, maybe he was becoming half-wild himself. I could picture him squirreling away tidbits in some clever hiding place, but instead of making me angry, the image squeezed a harsh giggle out of me.

Suddenly I recalled the hidden package of beans. I pried out the piece of log, and in the hole was one-half of a neatly broken chocolate-chip cookie—the one I had almost gotten killed going after. I laughed out loud.

"Yum, yum," I said. "No wonder Mister Skunk went into the bucket."

"That man," I sighed, putting the remnant of cookie back and closing the hiding place. "Mischief is his life."

I shuddered to think what sort of mischief he might be up to at this moment . . . nearly two o'clock on an unseasonably balmy winter's night. It hardly seemed worth fretting about, so I eased my over-tired body into bed and proceeded to thrash and twitch my way through several hours of restless, dream-riddled sleep.

Purple-gray clouds clogged the morning sky, and without sunstreaks across my room to waken me, I slept later than usual. Breakfast was a plentiful affair compared to recent slim pickings, but lonely without

Dick at the table sipping coffee in his quiet morning way.

There was plenty of work to occupy my time, and after gathering all the soiled clothes and linens I started the washing machine. When it came unbolted halfway through the spin cycle and started to jiggle across the floor, I discovered the heavy-duty screwdriver was missing from Dick's toolbox.

I walked down to the toolshed to search for a screwdriver. I had never really looked around in that building before, and now I saw that it was a marvel of order and completeness. Every tool imaginable either hung on the wall or reposed in neat rows on two long workbenches. In the midst of all this perfection an oddity stuck out, and when I had located what I was looking for, I walked back to the corner where the thing was propped.

Perplexed by its apparent uselessness, I stood staring at it. Basically it was a pole with a shoe attached to one end . . . one of Dick's old black loafers, it looked like. I picked it up and saw that there was something nailed to the sole of the shoe—some sort of wooden contraption with five . . . digits? *Toes?*

A scream like a siren ululated from my throat.

"The Bigfoot tracks . . . he made them with *this!*"

My howling turned to laughter as I pictured Dick wielding the pole, a look of grim concentration on his face while he made footprints as though his very life depended upon it.

I put the contraption back exactly where I had found it. Never in this world would I let on that I had

discovered his secret. Maybe someday I'd make tracks
with it, and give Dick something to think about! Still I
didn't rule out the existence of the Sasquatch, and
what better place for them to roam than this valley?

9
Fetching
Dick Home

The day passed quickly as I scrubbed and cleaned, taking frequent breaks because I was out of condition after the long weeks of being housebound. I was ready for bed by nine o'clock, and slept like a stone until awakened by the shrill ringing of the telephone.

"I have a collect call for anyone at this number from a Richard Lowe. Will you accept the charges?"

"Yes, of course," I said, wondering if Dick was so messed up he had forgotten my name.

"Hello, honey? It's me ... Dick. I'm up at Elmo—you'll have to come get me."

He hung up with a bang. I stared at the receiver for a moment, and then hung it back on the wall. So where was Elmo? And how would I find him, when I got there? I glanced at the old Seth Thomas octagonal clock, which read 4:38 A.M. A popular time for heart attacks, I was sure, as I bumbled around starting coffee and searching for a map.

"Ought to let him get back home the same way he got to *Elmo*," I grumbled. "That's why he hung up so fast, so I wouldn't have a chance to refuse."

When I was dressed and ready to go, I discovered that the key hanging on the gas tank hook would not unlock the tank. Muttering oaths about careless people, I was forced to try over a dozen of the keys on the big ring before I located the right one and could fill the truck's tanks.

By the time I pulled out, the sky above me was as luminous as a polished pewter bowl and my grumps had dissipated. I drove carefully over the mountain, drinking coffee from my thermos as I watched the world come alive for another day. There was very little traffic on the freeway at that hour, mostly the big eighteen-wheelers hurtling their loads toward the Coast, so I made good time. Somewhere between St. Ignatius and Ronan the sun burst over the mountain and poured light across the land and my spirits soared. Whatever Dick had done, it would not change our lives. He was coming home with me.

There had been no need to worry about where I'd find him. I cruised down the main drag of the little burg and there he was, big as life and dirty as sin, lying on his back on a bench in front of an unprepossessing beer joint. An old Indian in a greasy fringed vest squatted beside him, plucking at the beadwork on his moccasins as he listened to something Dick was saying.

Hearing the truck idling at the curb, Dick got stiffly up and limped over. A low moan escaped his lips as he hoisted himself into the cab, whether from the effort or in greeting I wasn't certain. I sat speechless, surveying the odiferous wreck that was Beartracks Lowe after a wing-ding. There was a long smear of blood across his forehead, but no wound that I could see.

I made a tight U-turn and headed back south, and in

a few minutes Dick had slumped over against the door and was snoring in long rattling inhalations, like an ancient tractor in need of a tune-up. When I stopped in Arlee to eat he reared up and stared wildly around, his eyes unfortunately falling on a mural of an abundant breakfast painted on the side of the restaurant. By some ghastly trick of sun or pigment, the egg yolks had turned a violent puce green and the ham lavender, a sight which made Dick's face go so gray and clammy that I changed my mind about offering to bring him coffee.

He was snoring when I returned, and we were almost to Missoula before he stirred again, flapping his hands around as though insects were tormenting him.

"SHUT that window," he yelled, "you dirty rotten . . . oh! It's you, Jenny. Forgive me. I mean excuse me. I don't ask anyone but the Lord for forgiveness. But I'm cold, so awfully cold."

He shivered so violently the seat trembled, and I turned the heater up as far as it would go.

"I'm a very sick man," he said, rubbing at the mud caked down his left side *cap a pie.*

I didn't doubt it for a minute.

"I feel things too deeply," he went on, voice scratchy. "These emotions have played hob with my body . . . wrecked it, if the truth be known."

My mind fragmented, scurrying in all directions to locate a memory riveting enough to block out his painful words, like the time I won the county spell-off, or the first time I made love stretched out nude in a bed. Nothing worked—there was no escaping that voice. It droned on like an old bull too weak to bellow, its lowing vibrating with sorrowful resonance.

"One of my wives—a beautiful young girl—disappeared, and I never did find out what happened to her. I even put an ad in *Life* magazine with her picture, in case anyone had seen her. It's terrible not knowing if your loved one has met with foul play or just decided to take off. And coming on the heels of having to bury the one . . ."

His mouth snapped shut so fast I heard his teeth click.

"Oho," I thought, "we get to the main one at last. The one who ran off may have been young and possibly even beautiful, but the one who died was his soulmate."

Dick began to drum his fingers on his knee and I noticed gunk under his nails, as though he'd been eating mashed potatoes and gravy with his hands. He waved a finger under my nose and growled,

"You're pretty high strung yourself, kid! Better learn to control your feelings, before dryrot sets in from head to foot."

I spoke for the first time since Dick had gotten into the truck, "Well, I'm trying."

He stiffened and stared straight ahead, as though the sound of my voice had returned him to a reality he would prefer not to face.

"Maybe it's better to be able to feel something," I added softly, "than to be a . . . robot. There are already plenty of those in the world."

We stopped in Missoula to exchange the loaner for Dick's truck. If the garage personnel were shocked by his appearance, you couldn't have told by their faces.

Dick fumbled a credit card out of his wallet to pay for the repairs, and as soon as we were under way again he went back to sleep. When we were halfway up Monkey Mountain he snorted and said,

"You woke me up, grinding your teeth! Just relax, can't you? Don't think about the road being slick as snot on a doorknob, and stop sneaking looks over there where it drops off like a chute straight to Hell . . ."

"Oh, be quiet," I said. I didn't need any reminders about those drop-offs.

In his usual effort to have the last word, Dick said,

"You smell like you had a run-in with a skunk."

The last of my patience died.

"Well good! Then we're even!" I yelled in his ear, causing his head to snap back. "There's no animal on earth that stinks as bad as you do right now!"

That held him until we got to the cabin, whereupon he tried to go directly to bed.

"Oh no you don't," I said. "You need some food in your belly. Look at that."

I grabbed his belt and pulled out on his pants, and it looked like his stomach had shrunk six inches. I set out cold sliced beef, bread, pickles, and hard-boiled eggs, and re-heated the leftover coffee. When he had finished, I made him take a shower.

"Aw, nuts," he sputtered, too weak to resist my tugging and shoving. "Two baths in one week? This is total *insanity!*"

Dick was a sick and sorry man next day. I thought he was going to die, and maybe he almost did. Winter closed in again, as he had predicted. Below zero temperatures returned, and vengeful howling winds brought one blizzard after another.

Dick remained unusually subdued, and one day he produced a gray metal box I hadn't come across in my browsing. He unlocked it with a small brass key and asked me to sit down beside him.

"I know you love the life we live up here," he said.

"Yes I do," I replied. To deny it would have been a blatant lie.

"You have treated me very well," he continued in somewhat formal tones. "Better than most. And I think highly of you . . . admire your . . . many good traits."

Voluble Dick was unable to dredge up any more words, and I could think of no way to help him along. Pink blotches bloomed and burned on my cheeks.

"Maybe we met for a purpose," he said at length, and a document he had taken from the strongbox quivered in his hands.

"You seem to thrive on quiet—could you ever live in a city again?"

"Why, I don't know," I said, wondering uneasily what all this was leading up to. "I suppose maybe I'll have to . . . someday."

My uncertain words washed the expression from his eyes until they were flat as river stones, and he mumbled,

"For time and chance happeneth to them all."

"A Bible quotation?" I asked. "I didn't realize you were a religious man, Dick."

"No one could live in a place like this and not believe there's a God," he said softly.

In the long moments of silence that followed, the ticking of the clock grew louder as my hearing grew more acute, as it always did just before I got one of those spooky spells that presaged an *event.* Then Dick's words came rushing out, fairly tumbling over each other.

"I've got a cabin and . . . uh . . . and some . . . oh, about ten acres. Up at Swan Lake."

"Yes?" I prompted.

"I want to leave the place to you."

I sat frozen with shock, but Dick must have seen the questions in my eyes.

"I'm hardly past my prime, Jenny, but already I'm worn out. It was too hard—do you know what I'm saying? Just too almighty blasted *hard!* My guts are telling me my time is about up."

"Oh no . . . oh no, Dick," I whispered. "I'm sure you'll have many years yet." But my hopeful words could not erase his declaration. Dick sighed and looked out at the land he loved, and guilt prodded at me as I wondered if he had been seeing a doctor on some of the occasions when I'd been so sure he was out tomcatting. His eyes swung around and fastened on mine with a terrible intensity and he said,

"I don't want it to happen in town."

There didn't seem to be any possible reply to that, and after a moment I said,

"I didn't know you owned property."

"Several parcels," he said, shoving a handful of papers at me, which I didn't look at. "Don't worry, my kids will be well taken care of. But who cooks my food, looks after the house, listens to me bellyache when I'm drunk? In other words, girl, who takes care of me? You are the one here with me . . . right?"

I blinked back the moisture threatening to spill from my eyes. Dick saw, and took my hand and held it for a long time, and then he said,

"When this weather breaks, let's drive over the mountain and get hitched. Want to?"

"I thought you'd never ask," I said.

There seemed no reason to tell anyone we were now officially united, since common-law marriage was—and is—legal in Montana. Our brief ceremony hadn't really been necessary, but Dick was set on it, and I'll have to admit it changed us both.

Operating under the delusion that he was now less likely to throw me out, I began to give full play to all the half-repressed aspects of my personality. There was Jenny the loudmouth (long denied voice—or at least equal time), the seductive tease, the roughneck, the blue sobber, and the childish one who shrieked with delight when the wilderness yielded up its treasures. Yes, there were many Jennys, and Dick accepted them all, though it was hard to tell if he liked the change.

For his part, the metamorphosis took longer, but I gradually comprehended that a good part of his *persona* had been an act . . . a boisterous bluster to conceal the nice man inside. Tiny chinks appeared in his armor and grew larger by the day, and before long we almost seemed to be exchanging natures—I becoming more the

carefree joker, while Dick developed a measure of tran-
quillity—even spending some time in thoughtful meditation rather than talking rattledy-bang all day long.

It was beginning to seem that spring would never
favor our high lonely retreat with its arrival. I bundled
up in the same old heavy clothes, shivering until the
sun climbed over the mountain to give an impression of
warmth which the thermometer failed to back up.

Then in the space of a few days a maddeningly
balmy scent began to creep into the air, and the small
hard buds on the trees unfurled into lush green leaves.
Before a week had passed the meadow stretched out,
not in bridal white, but like a field of emeralds sprin-
kled with yellow buttercups and dotted with bright
spots that soon blossomed into scarlet Indian paint-
brush flowers.

The only worry marring this idyll was the speed with
which the mountains were changing their aspect. As we
drove to Clinton one day, I spoke to Dick about it.

"Don't you think the snowpack is coming off way
too fast? You can almost see the difference from one
day to the next."

Dick cuffed me on the shoulder and said, "You're a
pretty neat kid, you know that?" Strange reply.

I hit him back, a little harder than I intended to.
Maybe we weren't your average married couple, but
our misalliance had its moments, and I had learned to
love him deeply—probably inevitable considering our
shared good times and our dependence upon one
another. Sometimes, in fact, I was afraid I cared for Dick
more than I wanted to. Past experience having taught

me that total love brings pain in the same degree, I had tried to hold a part of my heart in reserve. Still, I was happy, and as for Dick—well, who ever knew what was truly in the heart of a man?

I forced these imponderables from my mind. The day was far too fine to waste on perplexing riddles, or to worry about the melting snow that even now must be hurtling into the tributaries that fed the creeks and rivers of our valley, swelling them to dangerous volumes.

We stopped at the Post Office for the mail, which contained several personal letters in addition to the usual junk. One of them was from my oldest son, and when I opened the envelope a shower of apple blossom petals cascaded onto my lap.

"Uh-oh," I said. "They must be trying to tempt me to go down there and help out with the new baby."

"You won't go, will you?" Dick asked anxiously. "Maybe next year."

"No, I won't go," I said. "After all, I have a new husband."

That got me a peck on the cheek, and then he said,

"They're coming early this year."

"Who? You don't mean the boss and his family?"

He nodded, and I struggled to conceive of our secluded Eden crawling with people.

"But what *for?*" I said crossly. "What about all the trips we planned—like to Garnet and to visit Mary? And you promised to take me across the Skalkaho and along the Lochsa."

Dick's eyes began to twinkle, and I knew it amused him that I was now every bit as jealously possessive of the ranch as he was. Still my feeling of annoyance grew, even though I knew it was patently unreasonable. After all, they *owned* the place.

"We'll have to put off some of those jaunts until later in the year," he said. "Still some good weather left, after they leave—most years, anyhow."

He handed me a shopping list that had been enclosed with the letter.

"This is your department," he said. "You've played all winter—soon be time to work."

"What do you mean . . . *work?*"

"Oh, it's an easy job helping the cook. You'll still have time between meals to take your hikes, and what-ever you do out there."

"But why haven't you told me this before?"

"Why, I sort of thought you'd have figured it out. Place like this, there's usually a man and wife, and they both work."

Some of the brightness went out of the day as I digested this unwelcome lump of news. A little bird whispered *you've been had* into my ear, and it took all my will power to keep from lashing out at Dick.

Closing my mouth firmly, I tried to hold at bay the bad thoughts and feelings. Dick might be replaced if he didn't have a partner . . . was that why he had latched onto me? Had I made another mistake by not returning to my Bible Belt homeland—a place I had never wanted to leave?

Gentle memories of the family farm drifted into my mind, easing out the anger. I closed my eyes, and my imagination paraded a succession of honest faces—

people I had known in my growing-up years—serious, plain-spoken, simply dressed folks who shared my values, and whose word was their bond. Then it came to me that I would be trying to return to an *era*, not a place . . . a time which had passed. It would be like trying to embrace a ghost.

As we neared the cabin there was a low rumbling sound like the roll of thunder, although the sky was clear.

"Rocks coming down the river," Dick said soberly. "You were right, honey, it's a fast melt—too fast. The cabin will be safe, high up as it is, but we'll have to keep a close watch on the rest of it."

The river continued to rise, and a week later I decided to get the jump on things by purchasing the canned and frozen items on the shopping list the boss had sent. The produce could be picked up the day before they arrived.

I stood at the sink filling the coffee pot and gazing out the window. Sometime during the night the river had spread out all over the meadow, and was scooting boulders around like a giant boy shooting marbles with wild abandon. Dick was still asleep after a restless night, so I didn't wake him. If the low spots in the road were already flooded, I would just have to turn around and come back.

Since it seemed prudent to get an early start, I dressed quickly and limited my morning meal to toast and coffee. I crossed the mountain without incident, and as I locked the gate to the ranch behind me, a bent figure came out of the trees and walked up the road toward me. It was the pensioner who lived in a cottage on the nearest farm.

"Hi, Papa Pete," I called.

"Hello missy," he said, approaching the truck at his slow shambling gait.

"What do you make of all this water that's rushing around?"

"Bad . . . very bad," he said, and there was none of the usual merriment in his dark eyes. "Whole buncha big trees coming down the river now—see 'em? A big tangle of 'em's stuck under the bridge. But they got to go sometime, and when they do—*ka-blam!* Might take the whole bridge out."

"I'm afraid you're right," I said. "Take care, now." I went on, horrified at the mass of uprooted trees pressing against the bridge, and as I drove across it I could feel the wooden planks shake with the force of the water rushing against the pilings. The skin behind my ears was tickled by the first vestige of a prescient feeling. Something bad was building, and building fast, and nothing in this world could stop it.

I soon regretting having come to the market without Dick. Many of the items on the list were things we never bought, and it seemed to take me forever to search them out. Halfway through my chore, a sudden urgent need to return to the ranch propelled me to the checkstand, where the clerk eyed the many gourmet foods and remarked,

"Looks like the Finnegans are on the way. Think they'll get here before the bridge washes out?"

"I don't know what to think," I said. "This is my first year here."

"Is that a fact? Well, watch out for that Rock Creek. It's a killer, and we've lost some good people to it."

As I drove out of the parking lot, raindrops rattled on the windshield.

"Just what we don't need," I groaned, pulling to the curb to transfer the groceries from the truckbed into the cab. I dreaded to think what effect this additional water would have on our already volatile situation.

The shower increased and I was streaming water by the time I had everything stacked on the passenger seat and floor. I started for home, shaking with chills and driving as fast as I dared on the stormswept highway.

I saw that the bridge had held and heaved a sigh of relief. But halfway across I slammed on the brakes and skidded to a stop, for there was nowhere to go—the river had broadened out into a rolling sea covering the road almost to our gate, and its dark brown color indicated that it had already dug a deep channel.

Three barely visible people stood on the far side of the floodwaters, and when the rain slackened I saw that they were Dick and the farmer and his wife. Della was holding one of her horses, and bobbing in the water before them was an aluminum rowboat. Slackjawed with amazement, I watched as she tied a rope to her saddle, secured the other end to the boat, and started to swim the horse across the river towing it. The animal behaved as though he had always dreamed of performing that feat, eyes rolling, head tossing, full of himself, as well he might be. Unfortunately they hadn't counted on the volume of groceries I had.

Her husband had hopped into the boat at the last minute. He greeted me with a rueful grin, and we started loading the bags.

"You'll have to make two trips," I said, as the boat sank low in the water under the weight of the canned goods.

"Yep, and we'd better get a move on," he said. "This bridge is going to go, all right. It's just a question of when."

They started back across and all went well until about midstream, when the rope broke and boat began to spin in ever faster circles. Suddenly it was sucked out of the maelstrom and shot straight toward a huge culvert. Just before it was swept into the yawning hole, the boat turned over, tossing cans into the sky like a flock of cylindrical birds. I scanned the current for a corpse, but when the boat popped out the other end Della's husband appeared, holding up two fingers in a victory sign.

"Victory at sea," I muttered. "Well, he's lucky to still have his head attached to his body."

He tumbled along in the wild water, sometimes completely submerged, and finally grabbed hold of a cottonwood tree that hadn't yet been uprooted. There he clung until Della swam her horse over to rescue him.

The boat was nowhere in sight, and I experienced a wonderful feeling of relief that operation horse-taxi had been brought to a halt. Now I could drive back to town and check into a warm, dry motel, get out of these sopping clothes, have a hot bath, *eat.* Fortunately, for it was the most expensive part of the order, the meat was still in the truck. It could be put in a locker overnight, or however long it took Mother Nature's fit to run its course. I started the truck and put it in reverse, and then came a faint cry which I barely heard over the roar of the river, and wished I hadn't. "Wait . . . wait!"

There they came again, plucky woman and horse, bringing the boat, which must have washed up somewhere.

"Well, you could pretend you didn't see them," I told myself, but no, it wouldn't have been sporting at all, and some might even have called it downright chicken.

Quickly loading the rest of the sacks, I glanced at the knot where Della had tied the ends of the broken rope together . . . rather carelessly, it looked to me. By the time I backed the truck off the bridge I was trembling with anxiety, which increased when I stepped into the now-battered boat and felt the terrible strength of the river through the thin aluminum skin separating it from the soles of my feet. It throbbed and drummed and I sang to myself a funeral dirge which went thusly:

"That Jenny is a fool—a truly hopeless imbecile who insists on doing someone else's idea of the *right thing.* She'd better recite her prayers, and get ready to say howdy to the culvert."

Della gave the culvert a wide berth and plenty of new-found respect, and we reached the other side safely. Dick helped me out of the boat, and I noticed that he too was dripping wet.

"What happened to you?" I asked.

"Aw, I slipped and fell in," he said sourly. "Lost my favorite hat, too."

"Oh no! Not your red baseball cap?"

He nodded glumly, and we began to transfer what remained of the groceries. Dick's special cap gone—it ranked right up there with the worst of the day's catastrophes.

10
The River Changes Course, and Time Changes Everything

I woke several time in the night, listening to the roar of rain as it beat down on the roof, and thinking somber thoughts about how totally all living creatures are at the mercy of the elements. A gauzy gray light had just begun to filter into the room when Dick called,

"That river's gone hog-wild! I'm going out to check the road. Maybe you'd better come along."

I slipped out of bed and went to the window. The valley was an unrecognizable crazy-quilt pattern of new riverbeds, boiling like cauldrons and tossing rocks around. What had formerly been Gilbert Creek now contained but a trickle of water, and as I watched, horrified, its banks began to cave in.

"Oh my Lord," I murmured, "maybe the cabin is going to go, after all."

When I went into the kitchen, Dick was standing transfixed at the window.

"Never saw anything like it," he said, "and I've lived in Montana all my life."

I dumped some coffee into a Thermos jug to drink along the way, and as soon as we got around the first bend we could see that a section of the road was already under water.

"Are you going to try to drive through it?" I asked.

"Nope. Can't take the chance . . . might be deeper than it looks. Even if we made it, it might be a lot worse by the time we come back, and we'd have to swim home. I brought a couple of shovels, and we'll do some ditching right now."

We dug several trenches to drain the road, and then proceeded over the mountain. On the other side, we had to do more ditching to reach the gate.

"Look, Della's still bringing people across the river in her boat," I said.

"One of them's Danny," Dick replied, gazing at the two figures crouched in the boat. "Can't be anything but bad news."

Danny stepped out of the boat and hurried over to us. "Did you know your power's out?" he asked.

"Oh no," I groaned, "all that meat I put in the freezer at the lodge! And the things in our refrigerator."

"We didn't know," Dick said, shrugging as though to settle this new burden onto his shoulders. "Left early, to dig some channels . . . get this floodwater drained off of the road."

"It'll be all right for a couple of days," Danny assured us. "Just don't open the freezer door."

He looked exhausted, his forehead striped with frown lines and brackets of tension around his mouth.

"Here's the situation," he said. "The bank collapsed on the other side a couple of miles upriver. The pole washed away and of course the line snapped. We got a new pole up, but the water's too wild there to take the new line across. Don't have a partner working with me now, either . . . so many emergency calls coming in, we had to split up."

"Rough," Dick said darkly, "rough as a cob. Got any ideas?"

"Well, I might have. If you want to go up there, I'll go back across and try to cast the line over to you with a fishing rod. It's worth a try."

We drove upriver to the new power pole, and in a short while Danny appeared on the other side and started casting. The line fell into the water several feet from the bank.

"Why don't you get that rope out of the Bronco, and tie it around my waist?" I asked. "I could hop in and grab that wire."

"Are you crazy?" Dick squawked. "At the speed that water's traveling, I wouldn't be able to hang onto you. Come on, we might as well go."

He turned away just as a huge raft-like clump of logs and debris got hung up on some rocks near the bank. Danny was still casting, and practice was improving his aim. The line smacked the water a foot from the mass of floating logs, and without a second thought I jumped onto it. Dick screamed something unintelligible as I hooked one foot over a log and leaned out to grip the wire. A second after I leaped back ashore, the log jam broke up and rushed downstream in a million pieces.

Danny came back across the river to hook up our new power line. "Good work, you guys," he said.

"You too, Dan," Dick responded. "I wouldn't have your job at any pay . . . at least not this time of year! Say, who came across in the boat with you?"

"That's your new cook. She's waiting for you to take her up to the ranch."

Dick looked utterly confounded, and after a minute Danny added, "They told her to clean the lodge, she said . . . and you're supposed to break her in. That's why she came on ahead of the others. I . . . uh . . . I guess they didn't know you already had someone up there with you."

It was the first I'd heard that Dick had never told the Finnegans about me, and I cast about for some logical reason for his silence. Was he still in doubt that I would stay, even now that we were married? Or was he just keeping his options open so he could make a quick switch if something better came onto the scene?

We drove back to the gate where a young woman with long brown hair stood shivering. Her jeans were sopping wet, and from the expression on her face, I judged that she might turn out to be one of the short-timers.

"You must be Mister Lowe," she said. "There's a leak in that darn boat, and I got wet. So did everything in my tote bag."

She kicked at a sodden piece of canvas luggage beside her. Then she looked at me.

"This is Jenny," Dick said. "She's going to help you. And what was your name?"

"Just call me Annie."

"Welcome to Valley of the Moon, Annie," he said, "and don't worry about your wet things—there are a couple of dryers up there."

Somehow I ended up in back with the luggage, while Dick proceeded to coax Annie out of her hostile mood.

It wasn't long before my previous thought about Dick's bravado having concealed a nice man had burned to bitter ashes.

"Sure, real nice," I told myself. "So soft-hearted, he just can't bear the thought of a woman alone."

Our branch of the creek had crested, and when we reached the plateau I saw that one of the brand-new tributaries had won out and become the new bed for Gilbert Creek. Some half-dozen others had subsided and were already starting to dry up. The scene had a pastoral serenity, but there was nothing peaceful about my frame of mind. Dick had whipped around one of the switchbacks too fast, sliding Annie over against him, and she had remained brazenly at his side. As he sat grinning like an egg-sucking fox, I saw with a painful flash of clarity that marriage had not changed him one iota.

"People don't change," I thought dully, "only the cast of characters and the scenery."

Back into my mind ambled a dark premonition I'd had that morning, forgotten during the exciting events of the day, and with fatalistic resignation I watched it begin to come true.

When we reached the cabin I went directly to my room, intending to change the bedclothes and move my things so that it would be ready for Annie's occupancy. I would be sleeping in the other twin bed off the kitchen during the summer months.

Once in the safety of the space that had become dear to me I found that I was too upset to do anything, and in fact it took some stern talking-to just to keep myself from flying into a jealous rage.

Finally my equilibrium returned, and with it a sharp pang of hunger. I went into the kitchen to fix myself a meal. As I lingered at the table, I considered the possibility that this hectic day, with no food until mid-afternoon, had played hob with my body chemistry or blood sugar or something, causing me to imagine all these silly things. Before long I'd done such a good job of convincing myself, I actually went down to the lodge and offered to help Annie with the cleaning.

"Oh, there's no need for that," she said. "*Dick* is helping me. He's already showed me where everything is."

After that exchange she turned sullen and would speak no more. I wondered uneasily if the boss or his wife had interviewed this strange girl in person . . . probably not, and as Dick had said many times, they were fortunate to get anyone. I went for a hike, and when I returned to the cabin Dick was sitting at the table cleaning one of his handguns.

"Guess I'd better get my clothes out of that bedroom," I said, "so she can move in."

"Don't bother," Dick said airily. "Annie's not used to living in a house with other people. When I was showing her around, she saw that tent stored up on the rafters of the garage—wants to pitch it in the clearing down by Spooky Springs."

"Huh . . . what is she," I said, somewhat taken aback, "some kind of nature girl?"

"No more than you," he said, "and the two of you will get along fine . . . just give yourself a little time to get acquainted."

I had serious doubts about that. The lump of foreboding that had formed in my breast when the three of us were in the Bronco returned, and I was quite sure no amount of lecturing myself would rid me of it this time.

Two days later, at a few minutes before midnight, I was wakened by the crunch of footsteps on the gravel road. I got up to find that Dick was not in bed, and wondered uneasily if he could be taking a walk, this man who hated to walk. I opened the door and looked up and down the road, saw that the Bronco was gone, and tasted the sickening prelude to impending endings.

"Pushed it a long way down the road before he started it," I muttered. "Thought he could leave without waking me . . . cheap trick, old boy."

It was the same stunt my oldest brother had pulled while sparking a town girl, and no amount of punishment had been sufficient to deter him. The actions of a teenager in the throes of a crush.

I stood in the road watching the moon skim the treetops, and considered sourly the day Dick had told me he didn't have long to live and had asked me to marry him. He certainly seemed robust enough now, and I couldn't help thinking he'd had some other reason for wanting to tie the knot, aside from making sure I was around to assist the cook, of course. I went back to bed, lying sleepless as I wondered for the first time if his woman from down South had good reason to seek solace in alcohol. My heart was heavy with the knowledge that I might have to leave my wilderness paradise. I would stick it out as long as I could, though, because there was so much at stake, on my part, anyway.

A few days after Dick's midnight excursion, I went down to the garden hoping to relieve my growing tensions by hoeing the weeds around our newly sprouted vegetables. As I passed the lodge, I glanced into the kitchen window and saw Dick and Annie sharing an embrace. I watched as they kissed. At first it felt as though someone had punched me in the gut, and then came the slow burn of a deep anger bearing no resemblance to my usual flash-in-the-pan blowups. But I needed to be positive, so when Dick returned to the cabin, I asked him point-blank if he and Annie were having an affair.

"I never said I was an angel," he said.

"Does that mean yes?" I persisted.

He shrugged and looked past me out the window, as though it were of no significance. My face was hot and my hands shaking, but I wasn't ready to put it to rest. I had taken vows with this man, and if there was any conceivable explanation, I intended to hear it.

"So our marriage meant nothing to you," I said. "Just empty words and a meaningless gold band."

"It meant a lot more than you'll ever know," he said, "but it's not like the first . . . I mean, after so many . . . oh, I don't know how to explain it."

He had the dead calm demeanor of a cop who has seen too much, he could still feel, but couldn't get really hot about it.

"Is there something wrong with me?" I asked, hating the desperation in my voice. "It would help me to know, because I certainly don't intend to spend the rest of my life alone."

"No, of course not," he said. "Don't ever think that."

"Well, then," I said, "do you suppose you have . . . a problem?"

"If I do," he said, "so do a lot of other guys."

I was not concerned with a lot of other guys, only my husband. Then the brutal circumstances of the position I was in crashed past the protective barriers I had erected and I jumped up, sick and shaken.

"Well, I can't stay here," I said. "Do you know of anyone . . ."

"Yes," he cut in, looking at me as though I were already a stranger, or someone from far back in his past. "Yes, I know someone who would be glad to have your job."

Of course.

How little we know ourselves. I thought I had been well prepared, had steeled myself against Dick's infidelities so that I might continue with the lifestyle I loved. Not so. Something fierce and proud reared up inside me, mad as hell and not about to take it. Those other times had been brief interludes with shadowy, unknown women, but this latest was a matter of having the dirty linen waved right under my nose, twenty-four hours a day—a woman I worked under constantly throwing it in my face. No. I wouldn't stand for it.

Trip time again. Alberta is a nice province, and it contained friends I could visit if I needed moral support. In a fit of orneriness I had taken off in Dick's truck, and the farther I got from the ranch the more unreal everything began to seem. Open spaces have never charmed me, and there seemed to be far too many of them—nothingnesses sliced by roads straight as dies that went on and on, like perfectly straight black pencil lines stretching toward the edge of the continent.

On the second day a few oil derricks appeared, and some cattle. There were lovely mottes of trees and then at last a smear on the horizon that I was happy to see transmogrify into Rocky Mountain House.

My friends were of European background, and instead of sympathy, my tale of woe was met with hoots of derisive laughter. I was given to understand that the situation which so outraged me was of small consequence in their culture.

"You must consider the *whole* marriage," they counseled, and after the raw edge had worn off that first surprised flush of hurt and anger, their teasing lifted my spirits and I was forced to admit it was a proper tactic to use on a broken-hearted fool. The women encouraged their men to flirt with me, and social skills that hadn't been used since courtship days were dusted off. Before long I began to feel like a human being again, an attractive woman, almost, although I firmly resisted their efforts to fix me up with blind dates. What did I need with more men in my life, when I couldn't even handle the one I had?

I was offered a small trailer to stay in for as long as I wished, which I gratefully accepted. A lot of beautiful days began to slip past. It seemed as though I'd hardly watched the sun soar into the clear sky, done the chores assigned me, and visited with my hosts, before the corral posts sent purple shadows streaking across the yard and another long northern summer evening was upon us.

At first I spent a great deal of the solitary times going over my conundrum, weighing certain undeniable benefits against Dick's . . . weakness. But there was no logical solution, and my heart was strangely reluctant to make its wishes known. The day came when my mind had enough of this futile game and put it firmly aside. I lived in the moment, enjoying the pure air and hearty meals, the animals and children, and a certain joy in accomplishing my simple tasks. Their spread was, in its way, nearly as fine as the Finnegans', but for me there would never be anything to rival Valley of the Moon.

When the first winter gales began to scour the prairies, it seemed right to get into the truck and drive back to Montana. At times, barreling down those long empty stretches, I asked myself if I wouldn't be better off to find Annie well ensconced and myself the erring party in a divorce proceeding.

I almost crashed right into Dick on one of the curves. He was plowing snow, and we both came to skidding halts with about six inches between the snowplow attachment and the front bumper of the truck. I had to admit (though not to him) that I'd been driving much too fast on the narrow twisting road, in a sudden tearing hurry to get home. We had a good, if shaky, laugh over our close call. Nothing was said, then or ever, about why I had left, and we resumed our life together almost as though there had been no interruption.

Several years later, a fine autumn day found us clearing brush from a small hollow where the boss was wont to retreat for religious meditation.

"Jenny, don't stay here alone," Dick said.

I had turned to watch some magpies darting above the trout ponds, scolding in their raucous way. I thought I heard a cry other that that of the birds, and then the meaning of Dick's words slammed into my mind. Whirling, I found him on the ground with the light of life already gone from his eyes.

I wobbled the half-mile to the cabin and called for an ambulance. I didn't know how they would get through the gate, but the combination on the lock was now changed yearly, and shock had driven the new numbers from my mind.

Like a robot I took the ring of keys from behind the door and made the rounds for the last time. When all the buildings were securely locked I dropped the key to the cabin in my pocket to give Mary. They could take Dick's belongings out, and they could have the Swan Lake property too. I had never intended to claim it. It was sufficient knowing that Dick had been concerned about my future, and had once cared enough to try and provide me with a measure of security. Well, I had never believed such a thing existed, and certainly nothing had happened to change my mind.

When my trembling made it imperative that I sit down, I hauled a kitchen chair outside and slumped into it. The cabin still held too much of Dick's essence, disturbing me more than I could bear.

I wanted very badly to go back and stay beside him, but the place where he had gone down was out of sight of the cabin and the road, and I would need to show the ambulance crew where to go. So strong did the urge become at times that I was tugged from my chair, to walk a few steps and then pace back and sit down again.

"I miss you already," I whispered, "and you've hardly gone."

A gust of cold wind moaned past the cabin, raising goosebumps on my flesh, but the chill that seized my body was as nothing compared to the coldness seeping into my soul. When all was calm once more, mountain music drifted into the void—a whole chorus of voices this time: "His hat was cuffed back, his spurchains were chingin' . . ."

It swelled to a crescendo of such proportions that I thought I must be going mad, and then gradually diminished to no more than the soughing of the breeze in the pine trees. Then it ceased, and that was the last time the wild country ever sang its song to me.